The Brihadaranyaka Upanishad 101

A modern, practical guide, plain and simple

D1518460

by Matthew S. Barnes

Dedication

I dedicate this work to those who have the gumption to think for themselves. Such a feat is not easy, or accepted, in this world of ours.

I also dedicate this work to all those who have suffered at the hands of religious intolerance, in all its variants.

We all seem to desire the freedom to search for our own truths. We all seem to desire the freedom to worship and believe in our own ways. Yet many of us do not wish to grant the same religious freedom to others that we so earnestly and sincerely desire for ourselves.

Also by Matthew Barnes

1. **The Zen-nish Series:**
    (amazon.com/author/matthewbarnes)
    The Tao Te Ching 101
    Albert Einstein, Zen Master
    The Tao Te Ching 201
    Jesus Christ, Zen Master
    Dr. Seuss, Zen Master
    Willy Wonka, Zen Master
    Mark Twain, Zen Master
2. **Ancient Egyptian Enlightenment Series:**
    (amazon.com/author/matthewbarnes)
    The Emerald Tablet 101
    The Hermetica 101
    The Kybalion 101
3. **The Hindu Enlightenment Series:**
    The Upanishads 101 (broken into parts)
    The Bhagavad Gita 101
4. **Investing Series (Zen-vesting):**
    (amazon.com/author/matthewbarnes)
    Investing 101
    Investing 201
*   My investing style is controversial, but I have
    done very well with it. It is based around riding
    the rhythm of the market.

Contents

Foreword

I first came across the Upanishads while watching the 1984 version of *The Razor's Edge* starring Bill Murray. I had no idea the movie would have spiritual connotations, but it did, and I was hooked.

By the time I came across the movie, I had already studied many different religious and spiritual paths but was not yet familiar with the Upanishads. Ironically, I was already familiar with the *Bhagavad Gita*, a later Hindu text, but not its younger sibling.

The Razor's Edge originally appeared as a book by the same name. It was written by British author Somerset Maugham in 1944. The title comes from a line in the Katha Upanishad, which states, "the path to enlightenment is as hard to walk as attempting to balance upon a razor's edge." (paraphrased)

Maugham's storyline is a modern rendering of a tale found in the Upanishads. It follows a poor and pious man who seeks something more out of life after being changed by the horrors of World War I. If you have not seen either movie (there are two; one made in 1946 and one in 1984) or read the book, I think it would be well worth your time.

Though I came across them later in my studies, I discovered the Upanishads to be among the best-known philosophical/religious/spiritual works in the world and also among the oldest, predating the earliest known works of Greek philosophy. They are believed to be somewhere between four and five thousand years old and were initially transmitted orally. It was not until around 800–400 BCE that they began to be written down.

Each Upanishad is found at the end of one of the four main Vedas (or Hindu "Bibles")—the Rig Veda, the Sama Veda, the Yajur Veda, or the Atharva Veda—and their teachings, if set forth in one place, would encompass the length of an entire set of the *Encyclopedia Britannica*. They represent the summation of Hindu philosophy over generation after generation of contemplation and exploration into the physical and metaphysical realms of existence.

The Hindu religion, with its four "Bibles", compiled over an immense expanse of time, consists of such a wide variety of teachings and approaches that some critics have claimed it to actually be constructed of multiple religions that have, over time, converged into one.

The same can be said of other religions.

The Christian religion, for example, contains the Old and New Testaments, both of which have their own set of heroes, teachers, and lessons. These two Testaments differ so dramatically in overall tone that similar discussions have taken place among scholars (and even early Christians) over whether or not Judaism and Christianity are, in fact, two completely different religions, with two different Gods, that ended up converging into one.

The main difference between Hindus and Christians, at least in this regard, is that Christians tend to separate their Testaments. They tend to see the Old Testament as "history" and as a prediction of the coming of Christ. The New Testament is viewed as a fulfillment of these predictions and ultimately as a replacement of the Old.

Hindus take a different viewpoint. They seem to see all of their scriptures as a continuous thread of discovery, arguing that the subject matter is so vast, all-encompassing, and ultimately indescribable that variation in expression is unavoidable. Limiting ourselves to a single seer's description of what they experienced is like trying to figure out the overall image on a gigantic puzzle by only studying a single piece.

Critics do have a point though: the Hindu religion *has* evolved over time, it *has* changed. The earliest Hindus concentrated on a global focus of spirituality—they focused on nature. They saw evidence in nature of an Intelligence that transcended their understanding and observed, studied, worshipped, and prayed to this Intelligence in order to come to know It better.

The sun emerged from its slumber daily to bathe the world in warmth. The earth, the planets, and the stars were held in place by some unknown Force. All of nature, including humankind, seemed to be governed by never-ending cycles of birth, growth, decline, death, and rebirth. All that is was found to be held within a precise, unerring, and reliable order. In this they found their religion—a religion of nature—and proof to them of a mysterious Intelligence that created, animated, and guided all of life.

This is where the concept of Hinduism as a polytheistic

religion came from. On the surface, this seems valid. They did pray to the god of the sun, the god of the moon, the god of the wind, and so on. And they did give each god its own name. But ultimately, they believed all the different gods to be but the different characteristics, forces, and manifestations of the one God; each with their own individual duty to perform. One was the aspect of God that governed the sun. Another was the aspect of God that governed the moon. Still another was the aspect of God that caused the winds to blow, and so on.

This is very similar to the religion of the Native Americans who also revered and prayed to each individual aspect of God but recognized Wakan Tanka, the Great Spirit, as a single unified Whole that encompassed and included all the individual gods (or forces of nature). They too worshipped nature as evidence of a higher power and derived a great deal of peace from this viewpoint.

> *"When despair for the world grows in me and I*
> *wake in the night at the least sound in fear of what*
> *my life and my children's lives may be, I go and lie*
> *down where the wood drake rests in his beauty on*
> *the water, and the great heron feeds. I come into*
> *the peace of wild things who do not tax their lives*
> *with forethought of grief. I come into the presence*
> *of still water. And I feel above me the day-blind*
> *stars waiting with their light. For a time I rest in*
> *the grace of the world, and am free.*
> -Wendell Berry

Over time, as Hinduism progressed, the focus of their explorations into the Eternal changed. The seers realized the same Intelligence found in nature was also found within each individual.

This underlying Intelligence is what runs the processes and cycles of our bodies with unerring precision, just as It does with the forces of nature. It is what allows us to breathe and move. It is what spurs our hearts to pump, our food to digest, and our hormones to flow.

The Intelligence within each of us is also That which allows consciousness; that which allows awareness.

"Could this Intelligence be better pursued and discovered within the individual than in the study of nature?

"Can we contact this awareness? Can we become aware of the seer within each of us? Can we sense the hearer? Can we feel the feeler? Can we perceive the animator?

"This is the central theme of the Upanishads and the questions they aimed to answer. Can we become aware of That which lies within us that gives us life and consciousness? And if so, how?"

This change in focus from the global to the individual marks a major shift in Hindu exploration, one that eventually came to influence the central theme of Buddhism.

Buddha found enlightenment through the individual exploration of consciousness and came to believe the outer teachings to be a hindrance.

Learning the metaphysical construct of the universe (and our relation to it) seemed to incite endless intellectual and ego-centered debates on the meaning of the scriptures, along with the desire to worship the teachers that had delivered them.

Instead of traveling this route, Buddha found that excluding the external teachings and concentrating exclusively on the individual internal search was the quickest, most direct, and most prudent path; kind of a "cut-to-the-chase" route towards realization. Buddha was therefore well-known for refusing to answer questions about God, Heaven (Nirvana), or the structure of reality.

"I am trying to show you how to experience these things for yourself," he basically said. "Yet you want me to describe them for you instead. If I do, you will never find them. You will worship me, take my word for it, argue with others over what I meant, and forget to seek the answers for yourself.

"I will show you how to find It, but that is all. Find It for yourself, experience It directly, and then you can tell me about It if you wish."

As usual, I am paraphrasing.

When Buddhism made its way to China, it was combined with Taoism, which had similar beliefs, and became Ch'an. When Ch'an reached Japan, it became Zen.

The entire lineage, from the Upanishads down to Zen, is focused on this individual internal exploration and is another example of multiple religious beliefs merging, over time, into one, each one building on what had come previously, with new experiences and findings being added to the previous discoveries.

This, by the way, is how science, and all understanding, advances.

Where would we be if science refused, as many religions do, to advance?

We would still be living in huts, at best, without clean water, indoor plumbing, electricity, light bulbs, heat, or air conditioning. We would not have televisions, landline telephones, computers, cell phones, cars, airplanes, anti-biotics, or insulin.

We would still believe the earth to be flat, held up by "pillars", and the center of the solar system; nay, the universe. We would still believe that God lived, literally, just above the clouds of the earth, obscured from view by a thin layer of vapor. We would still believe, as did the early Christians, that all disease is caused by sin and sin alone.

Scientists who discovered that there were no pillars, that the earth was round, that there was no great bearded man floating above the clouds, and that the sun is the center of our solar system were tortured and killed by the Church.

Women who had knowledge of healing herbs were declared witches and burned at the stake or drowned. Again, sin was the only accepted cause of illness, and prayer was the only accepted cure.

The library of Alexandria, the storage facility for all ancient knowledge, was burned to the ground. Its curator was boiled in oil and his skin was scraped off with shells. The Christian who had this done was evidently sainted.

Why? Because the only truth the Church wanted

propagated was that which they found in the Bible. God created the world in six days, six thousand years ago, and then rested. And all disease was caused by sin. That is all we needed to know. All other possibilities were tortured or destroyed out of existence.

The Cathars, an early Christian group, is another example. They were completely annihilated by the early Catholic Church. Why? Because, according to the Cathars, Jesus came to teach us how to develop a *direct* relationship with God. There was therefore no need for churches or the paying of tithes. This is where the terms catharsis (a psychiatric method) and cathartics (laxatives) come from. It represents a complete and total eradication of bad thoughts (catharsis) or toxins in the bowels (cathartics). It represents the idea of completely eradicating something unwanted.

Three thousand years later, we have discovered atoms, harnessed the power of electricity, studied the quantum realm of existence, and even found new universes. This should not detract from our admiration for the underlying Intelligence of life; it should add to it, should it not?

The same can be said for advancing our understanding of God beyond that of a large, vengeful, bearded man into a formless benevolent Intelligence that created and still pervades existence.

Further, all that we have discovered since the time of Jesus, and all that we will in the future, was still created by this Intelligence, whether or not we were aware of it three thousand years ago.

Is evolution true? If so, it adds to the mystery of this

underlying Intelligence. Why? Because it would be much easier to create something once than to create it initially and then spend the rest of eternity fine-tuning it.

Is existence only six thousand years old or is it billions of years old, maybe more? If it ==does turn out to be more, once again, it would not detract from the mystery of existence or its creator. It would only add to it.

Why do we as a race so adamantly resist advancing our concepts of God? Forcing reality to fit into our current beliefs is very much like buying a shoe that is too small and then cutting our feet to make it fit.

> *"My dear Kepler, what would you say of the learned here, who, replete with the pertinacity of the asp, have steadfastly refused to cast a glance through the telescope? What shall we make of this? Shall we laugh, or shall we cry?"*
> **-Galileo**

> *"A scientific discovery is also a religious discovery. There is no conflict between science and religion. Our knowledge of God is made larger with every discovery we make about this world."*
> **-Joseph Taylor**

> *"All understanding passes through three stages. First, it is ridiculed. Second, it is violently opposed. Third, it is accepted as being self-evident."*
> **-Arthur Schopenhauer**

The focus on the individual search alone is so prominent in Zen that admiration for the messenger, or the outer teachings, is strictly forbidden. Such things, as Buddha taught, seem to hinder progress.

This is why pictures of the old Zen masters are always zany caricatures; they did not want anyone to get caught up worshipping them, the messenger, and miss the message, which is the only thing that is important.

> *"Do not seek to follow in the footsteps of the wise.*
> *Seek what they sought."*
> **-Basho**

This practice is in direct contrast to the way of Western religions, where belief or faith tends to be the central focus, along with the worshipping of the messenger, in place of seeking a direct experience with the Divine.

One Zen master, for example, when admired by a student once remarked, "Why admire me? All I can do is eat, sleep, shit, and piss. It is the Intelligence within you which allows you to do the same that you should be enamored with, not me."

Again, I paraphrased, but I remained true to the spirit of the teachings. The old Zen masters were often very direct and crass with their language.1

Apart from Buddhism, Cha'an, and Zen, the Upanishads also influenced Jainism and Sikhism as well as Socrates and other Greek philosophers.

They also influenced and formed the basis of the

philosophies and beliefs of Leo Tolstoy, Albert Einstein, Arthur Schopenhauer, Walt Whitman, Ralph Waldo Emerson, Henry David Thoreau, and President John Adams, just to name a few.

I cannot begin to express how influential the teachings of the Upanishads have been to our society. T.S. Elliot used the Brihadaranyaka Upanishad in his masterpiece, *The Wasteland*. The teachings of the Upanishads are even credited with forming the basis of the modern "New Age Movement" so despised by Western religionists.

> *"What lies behind us and what lies before us are*
> *tiny matters compared to what lies within us ...*
> *The eye cannot see it; the mind cannot grasp it.*
> *The deathless Self has neither caste nor race,*
> *neither eyes nor ears nor hands nor feet."*
>
> -Emerson

As Hindu thought and metaphysical experiences evolved even further (as I said, the Hindu lineage is very long), the two previous focuses of exploration—nature and the individual—were combined. You could find the Eternal by either means, they discovered, and they combined the two in the form of a summary of all previous findings. This summary was called the *Bhagavad Gita*.

Yet, the *Bhagavad Gita* is not simply a summary of previous beliefs, it also contains new findings, new revelations. Multiple paths to enlightenment were put forth and a path of devotion to a personified form of God was added to the previous non-personified paths as another valid route. For this reason, the *Bhagavad Gita* is commonly referred to as the "New Testament" of the Hindu faith.2

There are around 200 Upanishads but only ten to twelve (depending on the source) are considered primary. Most are from antiquity, but several were written much later. The primary ones, called the Mukhya Upanishads, will be the focus of these works. They are the most ancient, the most widely studied, and the ones that seem to best encapsulate the central ideologies of the Hindu faith.

Upanishad, roughly translated, means "sitting at the feet of the masters." Each one appears at the end of a Veda, at the end of one of the four Hindu "Bibles", not only as a final summary to each scripture, but also as a clarification of meaning.

Imagine being able to sit at the feet of Buddha, Christ, or any of the other great spiritual leaders and having the opportunity to ask them questions that would clarify the exact meanings of the scriptures. This is what the Upanishads are to the Hindus; they are nothing short of a kind of spiritual "question and answer session" between students and masters added to the end of each of the four Vedas.

The term Upanishad is also argued by some scholars to mean "connection" or "equivalence": All of life, the Hindus believe, is interconnected. The differences between all living things are superficial, not foundational, for we are all created from the same atoms, which are animated by the same unseen Intelligence.

All that is comes from the same "clay", so to speak, and is molded into different shapes and sizes. The only difference between a star and a heart, for example, is found in the pattern and vibrational signature of the atoms that have coalesced to create them. All else is the same.

The ancient Hindu seers claimed to have seen this interconnectedness. The ancient Egyptian seers claimed the same but explained it in their own way: "As above so below, as within so without. To know one is to know all."

At the heart of the Upanishads is what the Hindus refer to as Atman, the individual Soul, which is one with and connected to Brahman, the All-Soul.

This All-Soul creates the Universe, pervades the Universe, and *is* the Universe. It is the underlying unifying Intelligence of Life.

Ultimately, this view takes us beyond the idea of Hinduism as a polytheistic religion and into the realm of it being a "pantheistic" religion. Pan means all. Pantheism denotes the belief that God is all that exists.

Brahman, according to the Hindus, creates this existence out of Its own essence, animates this existence with Its essence, and therefore *is* the Essence of this existence. All that we see is but this Essence, this Energy, this Intelligence, manifested into different forms.

Notice I did not say that Brahman *created* the Universe but that It *creates* the Universe. Creation is not over for the Hindus. It is an ongoing process.

Atoms, cells, life forms, and even universes are constantly dying off and being replaced by new ones. Creation is therefore ongoing and evolving as Brahman, the underlying Intelligence of life, imagines, creates, explores, adapts, and evolves Its creation.

Put another way, this world was not created and then abandoned. It was not formed all at once by some kind of unfathomable Intelligence that then rested for the remainder of eternity. The Hindus see this Intelligence as a living entity that creates this world anew with every moment that goes by. It *is* life. It *is* gravity. It *is* attraction. It *is* the universe. It *is* death. It *is* rebirth. It *is* you. It *is* me.

Why does It create? Because It delights in doing so. It simply *loves* to, just as we do, for we were made in Its image. Not in form, but in mind—in Consciousness.

Just as our creations evolve, surpassing the creativity of our previous creations, so does Its. Where is the fun in creating the same old thing over and over? Hence the variety in life forms and the ever-evolving landscapes and moods of existence.

If forced to sum up the central theme of the Upanishads with a single quote, I would choose John 10:30, where Jesus declares, "I and the Father are One."

The ultimate lesson of the Upanishads is that God must not be sought as something far away, separate from us, but rather as the closest, most intimate aspects of our own being.

Discover Atman, your Soul, they say, and you will find It to be one with Brahman, the All-Soul, for you and the Father are One.

For many though, the word God has been stained. It

creates in them memories of organized religions that have often acted intolerantly with ignorance, hatred, and violence towards those outside of their faith. Try to keep in mind that this is the fault of humans and humans alone. They have even made God male, as can be seen by the use of the word Father in the previous quote.

For the Hindus, God is neither male nor female. It is beyond duality. It is beyond any and all concepts that the human mind can fathom. If you prefer, you can therefore substitute the word God with another term: Science, Consciousness, Energy, Force, or the underlying Intelligence of life, for example, which the Hindus sum up with the name Brahman.

This is one of the main reasons I have concentrated on the Eastern religions in my works. I would like those who have been put off by Western ideologies to see that there are other approaches, other ways of conceptualizing God; approaches they may be more comfortable with.

Whichever way works best for you is fine by me as long as it does not include intolerance in any of its guises.

For the Hindus, even science and religion are not at odds, for they are both simply attempting to understand the underlying thread of Intelligence that governs and binds all of life into all of its various forms and functions.

Both are attempting to understand the same thing, just from different vantage points. Both are valid and both are limited. Whatever this Intelligence is, It is beyond us. Combining these vantage points may bring us closer to actually conceptualizing the truth.

What follows is simply the Hindu attempt to explain, in human terms, their experiences with That which exists beyond the scope of the human mind and earthly senses.

The exact method of conception, they say, does not matter. The goal is to find a way, any way, that allows you to get a "feel" for That "which surpasses all understanding".

You must find the manner that works best for you. The Upanishads simply represent the method of conception that the long line of Hindu seers have found to best give them and those they were teaching this "feel".

As with my previous works, I have tried to simplify, modernize, and westernize the teachings of the Upanishads. My aim was not to create an academic, scholarly interpretation. Many of those already exist but may be difficult to digest for most readers. Instead, my aim was to deliver the "Big Picture" in a way that I believe most modern readers will find easier to grasp.

I left out the plethora of historical and cultural teachings that tend to confuse and discombobulate as well as the endless names and attributes of all the gods, concentrating instead on the core ideologies and beliefs.

Note as you read how similar the underlying themes of the Upanshads are to the ancient Egyptian teachings of my other works: *The Emerald Tablet 101, The Hermetica 101, and The Kybalion 101.* In fact, note how similar they are to many of the spiritual and religious teachings of the world.

Yes, you will find quite a bit of repetition in what follows. First, repetition is the mother of learning. One must hear something new over and over, in a variety of ways, before it begins to sink in.

Second, there are only so many ways to describe an idea, especially one that is, for all practical purposes, indescribable.

Third, most chapters (and many verses) are believed to have been contributed by different authors, each attempting, in their own way, in their own verbiage, to produce a deep understanding within their students. The central themes of Hindu thought are therefore often repeated but from varying perspectives.

One last thing: My interpretation is not an exact interpretation. It is not delivered as a word by word, line by line translation. It would be closer to the truth to say that my interpretation is *inspired* by *the Brihadaranyaka Upanishad*. As with my other works, I expound the central themes of the work, and remain true to the Spirit of its teachings, but I also expand on these beliefs with modern vernacular. The teachings are timeless. I feel that modern examples may give modern readers a better feel for the subject matter.

> *"The Upansihads are the production of the highest*
> *human wisdom and I consider them almost*
> *superhuman in conception. The study of the*
> *Upanishads has been a source of great inspiration*
> *and means of comfort to my soul. From every*
> *sentence of the Upanishads deep, original, and*
> *sublime thoughts arise and the whole is pervaded*

by a high and holy and earnest spirit. In the whole world there is no study so beneficial and so elevating as that of the Upanishads. The Upanishads have been the solace of my life and will be the solace of my death."
-**Arthur Schopenhauer**

See my works *The Tao Te Ching 101, The Tao Te Ching 201, Albert Einstein, Zen Master, and Jesus Christ, Zen Master* for more information on Taoism and Zen.

Consult my work *The Bhagavad Gita 101* for more information on its teachings. I believe it to be one of the most complete spiritual works in existence. It seems to cover just about every aspect of life and spirituality, including our struggles and the multiple paths we can take to overcome them and obtain freedom. It is both spiritual and practical in scope.

Reading Order

I initially planned on placing all twelve of the primary Upanishads into a single book. However, by the time I reached the halfway mark, the work was already well over 100,000 words.

I now plan to release them one at a time. I believe this will make them more appealing to the average person and easier to digest.

I will also release them in chronological order, at least to the best of my ability. The most ancient Upanishads are so old that their exact order is adamantly and continuously debated. The order I place them in is therefore going to be *generally* accurate but possibly not absolute.

Placing them in chronological order, I believe, will be simpler and may allow the reader to gain greater insight into the evolving understanding of the Hindus. Their newer teachings have never replaced the older ones, only added to them.

In any event, the chronological order I will be releasing these works in is, from oldest to most recent, as follows:

The Brihadaranyaka Upanishad
The Chandogya Upanishad
The Taittiriya Upanishad
The Aitareya Upanishad

The Kausitaki Upanishad
The Kena Upanishad
The Katha Upanishad
The Isha Upanishad
The Svetasvatara Upanishad
The Mundaka Upanishad
The Prasna Upanishad
The Mandukya Upanishad

There is another order in which the Upanishads may be read. In fact, classically, the following order is recommended for best understanding. This is the order that Hindu schools teach:

The Isha Upanishad
The Kena Upanishad
The Katha Upanishad
The Prasna Upanishad
The Mundaka Upanishad
The Mandukya Upanishad
The Taittiriya Upanishad
The Aitareya Upanishad
The Chandogya Upanishad
The Brihadaranyaka Upanishad
The Svetasvatara Upanishad
The Kausitaki Upanishad

I'd like to suggest you read the Upanishads in chronological order first then reread them in the classical order.

Keep in mind that the Hindus, like most other religionists, do believe their scriptures to be inspired by God, inspired by the experiences individuals have had with the underlying Intelligence of life that they refer to as Brahman.

But they also recognize that these experiences occurred within the limited minds of humans, who had great difficulty comprehending what they experienced and just as much difficulty explaining it.

These experiences were then passed down through the human race over long stretches of time, through scores of peoples who did not experience this Intelligence for themselves, thereby predisposing the teachings to some degree of variation in expression.

Further, as the human mind has evolved, so have the concepts and understandings by which we now interpret these experiences.

We all evolve. We are meant to. As we do, our ability to comprehend that which we previously could not expands.

"I am still learning."
-Michelangelo

"The human brain is still undergoing rapid adaptive evolution."
-Howard Hughes

*"The smaller your reality, the more convinced you
are that you know everything."*
-Thomas Campbell

Introduction

The Brihadaranyaka is most likely the oldest, and possibly one of the most important, Upanishads. It was written down somewhere around 800 BCE and placed at the end of the Yajur Veda.

Its name, loosely translated, means "Great Wilderness Teaching" or "Great Forest Teaching".

The work is typically credited to Yajnavalkya, an early Hindu Avatar (Messiah), though scholars believe it is more likely an accumulation of writings from several different contributors.

The Brihadaranyaka

Chapter One

1

The master thus explained creation, and the meaning of the statement, "Brahman is All," to his bewildered students:

2

"In the beginning, there was nothing but the One—That which many refer to as God.

"Many have attempted to describe It, many have attempted to name It, many have attempted to conceptualize Its nature in human terms, but all attempts have fallen short.

"No one really knows what It is. It simply cannot be fathomed by the human mind.

"Even those who have actually experienced It through near-death experiences, periods of intense suffering, the deepest states of meditation, or the deepest states of prayer have been unable to coherently put into words That which they experienced.

"Perhaps It can best be conceptualized as a vast field of Energy, a Force, a Great Mind, or Consciousness Itself.

"No. Even these concepts fall short.

"Still, they may be the best that we can do, for there are no other concepts in human experience that come as close.

"Except, perhaps, for the concept of love.

"Yes, comparing It to Love Itself also comes close.

"For simplicity's sake, we refer to It, whatever It is, as Brahman."

3

"The physical universe did not exist in the beginning. The 'Great Mind' had yet to stir. The material world had not yet become an idea within Its still waters.

"How long it had been that way no one knows. Time did not yet exist.

"What we do know is that It developed a yearning, a curiosity of sorts, a compulsion if you will; an impulse, a drive to create.

"At this point, it may help for you to think of Brahman as a perpetual state of Potential Energy, a perpetual state of stored-up energy, which has an innate drive to unwind, release, act, and produce."

4

"The pressure of this Potential Energy eventually built up to the point that It had to be released.

"A portion of the unified Whole, a portion of the One, succumbed to this pressure and was ripped into two opposing parts, two opposing poles: the male and the female, the positive and the negative, the proton and the electron, the 'yang' and the 'yin'.

"The result was a great explosion—what many refer to as 'The Big Bang'—as the opposing male and female energies burst forth from the One with the force of a trillion suns."

5

"Oil and water do not mix; their natures are incompatible. When poured together, they separate.

"In the same manner, the bipolar field of energy that burst forth from the rip in the fabric of the One was incompatible with the original, unipolar field. Thus did the two separate.

"The unipolar field remained as It was, but the bipolar field formed and filled a new reality, a new dimension: the dimension of duality, the dimension of time and space, the dimension of self and other.

"Thus are there two main dimensions or planes of existence: the dimension of the One and the dimension of duality."

6

"The dimension of the One is singular and without movement, change, or form. It is the cauldron of potential; the impetus for movement, change, and form; the will to experience movement, change, and form.

"The yang and the yin energies, on the other hand, attract and repulse each other in a nearly infinite number of combinations, creating the movement, change, and multitudes of forms we experience in the material world."

7

"Water, for example, is formed from two hydrogen molecules (which each have a single positive charge) that combine with a single molecule of oxygen (which has a net charge of negative two).

"Salt, on the other hand, is formed from a single molecule of sodium (which has a single positive charge) that combines with a single molecule of chloride (which has a single negative charge).

"Each molecule is seeking balance. Each molecule is looking to merge with its counterpart. Each molecule is looking to return to a state of wholeness, a state without division. Each molecule is looking to return to a state that is neither positive nor negative but neutral.

"Only in this state is it stable. Fractionated, it is not."

8

"The incessant, insatiable desire of the dual energies to reunite back into the One creates the movement, change, and forms we experience in this world.

"As these energies combine, dissipate, and reform, the seasons emerge, days ensue, and life forms are created and destroyed."

9

"As previously stated, there are two main dimensions. However, the dimension of duality is divided into multiple subdivisions.

"The original emanations of the Big Bang, the oldest emanations, those existing farthest from the One, have lost energy. Their rates of vibration have slowed and cooled, like the emanations of heat found at the outermost reaches of a fire. These energies have condensed, forming the elements of our realm, the most materially dense realm in existence. As these energies dissipate, the structures and life forms they created die off.

"The newest emanations, those just emerging from the One, those located closest to the blast site, were, and are, the most vibrant, the most energetic, like the emanations of heat located closest to a fire. They created, and still create (for the universe is still expanding, the Big Bang is ongoing), the most ethereal, the least dense dimension outside the realm of the One. The elements within its realm are very different from the elements of our own.

"Form, you see, is nothing but energy that is vibrating slowly enough that it takes on the appearance of form. The slower its rate of vibration the denser it seems. The faster its rate of vibration the less dense it appears."

10

"In between the most physically dense subdivision in material existence and the least exist layer upon layer, tier upon tier, stratum upon stratum of subdivisions, of subdimensions, each one vibrating on a level that is one octave higher than the last. Each one is a single degree less tangible than the last.

"Just beneath the least dense subdimension of physical existence, in a dimension of its own, resides the One."

11

"Have I given you the idea that these two dimensions, the dimension of duality and the dimension of the One, exist within two separate points in time and space?

"I hope not, for this is not correct.

"There is no such thing as time and space. It is an illusion, born of the dual energies of male and female, proton and electron, yang and yin.

"The two dimensions, along with the subdimensions held within the realms of duality, actually reside within a single point of Consciousness. They all reside within the mind of Brahman.

"The One is the Original Consciousness of Brahman. Material existence is nothing but Its thoughts, dreams, musings, and desires, which have been willed into existence."

12

"All about you, even now, at this very moment, lie the two main dimensions and all of the subdivisions, obscured from your perception only by the vibrational frequency of your own level of consciousness; the level of mind through which you perceive reality.

"Alter your level of consciousness, alter the state of mind through which you view it, and you alter your perception of reality."

13

"Protons and protons, and electrons and electrons, similar in energetic charge, repulse each other, creating, as I have said, the illusion of separation, the illusion of time and space.

"Protons and electrons, opposing in energic charge, clump together into atoms, creating the illusion of form, creating the illusion of independent identity.

"It is therefore the presence and interactions, the attractions and repulsions, between the male and female energies, the protons and the electrons, the yang and the yin that create the illusions of time, space, self, and other that we seemingly experience at this level of perception."

14

"There is no duality within the One. It is All and contains all. It is Consciousness Itself.

"There is no gender within the One. There is no male or female, no yang or yin.

"There is no direction within the One. There is no up or down, right or left, forwards or backwards, here or there.

"There is no time within the One. There is no before or after, no day or night, no summer or winter.

"Within the One, there is not even a distinction between self and other."

15

"The separation of the One energy into the two—the male and the female, the yang and the yin, the positive and the negative, the proton and electron—is what gives us the perception of gender in this realm. It is what gives us the perception of males (yang) and females (yin) as separate energies and entities.

"The separation of the One energy into the two—the male and the female, the yang and the yin, the positive and the negative, the proton and electron—is what gives us the perception of direction in this realm. It is what gives us the perception of an up (yang) and a down (yin), a right (yang) and a left (yin), a forwards (yang) and a backwards (yin), a here (yang) and a there (yin).

"The separation of the One energy into the two—the male and the female, the yang and the yin, the positive and the negative, the proton and electron—is what gives us the perception of time in this realm. It is what gives us the perception of a before (yang) and an after (yin), a day (yang) and a night (yin), a summer (yang) and a winter (yin).

(Now remains non-dual. It is within the Now that you may find the One.)

"The separation of the One energy into the two—the male and the female, the yang and the yin, the positive and the negative, the proton and electron—is even what gives us the perception of self and other within this realm."

16

"This seeming separation, as I keep saying, is an illusion. This world may seem solid, and it may seem to be separated into parts, but it is not.

"The smallest known building block of 'form' is the atom, yet the atom is created out of the two opposing wavelengths of energy that I keep referring to as protons and electrons, yang and yin.

At its most basic level, therefore, there is no form, only some kind of Energy that has slowed, clumped, and condensed into the appearance of form.

"Further, these two wavelengths of energy, the proton and the electron, are nothing but subdivisions of the *single* wave of Energy that we refer to as Brahman.

"Though all may seem separate, though there may seem to be a here and a there, a before and an after, a me and a you, all that exists is actually but an extension, a continuation, of a single field of Energy.

"The only thing separating me from being you, the air between us, or the ground below us, is the unique vibrational signature of our atoms. The atoms within my body clump and vibrate at a different rate than do yours, the air around us, or the ground below us."

17

"How do my atoms know to make me instead of you, or the air, or the ground? How do your atoms know to make you instead of me?

"How do the atoms that form your heart cells know to become heart cells, not brain cells or skin cells? The only answer is that this Energy we speak of is conscious, intelligent, aware; conscious, intelligent, and aware enough to have intent."

18

"This is why describing Brahman is so difficult. There simply is no single word that can encapsulate Its essence.

"The concept of Energy alone does not do it. Nor does the term Intelligence. Nor does the word Awareness.

"There are no words in any language that can encapsulate the full essence of what Brahman is.

"It is, at best, a combination of these concepts, yet even such a combination still falls short.

"Brahman is more than you can imagine, much less put into words."

19

"Keep in mind, though, that this appearance of separation exists as you know it only at this level of existence; only at your current level of perception.

"As you learn to transcend the material realm (in consciousness) the appearance of separation begins to blur more and more towards unity.

"The more deeply you are able to transcend your current level of consciousness, your current state of mind, the less separation you will experience."

20

"This unified construct of reality also explains why I say that Brahman is all that exists

"Brahman *is* the single field of Energy out of which all of existence, including protons and electrons, me, you, the air we breathe, and the ground we walk upon, is constructed, animated, and filled with consciousness.

"I am It. You are It. All that exists is It.

"We are all this Energy, vibrating at different rates, modes, and frequencies.

"The seeming separation we experience is illusory. At your current level of consciousness, your mind simply cannot perceive beyond this illusion."

21

"For simplicity's sake, we refer to this Energy as a whole as Brahman, or the All-Soul, and we refer to the portion of this Energy as It resides within each individual form as Atman, or the individual Soul.

"The world therefore comes from Soul and *is* Soul.

"What, then, is Soul?

"The simplest explanation is that It is the base substrate, the single field or wave of Energy out of which existence is constructed, animated, governed, and given consciousness."

22

"Even the physical world around you is more than you may imagine, for it is actually the material body of Brahman.

"Just as you have a body and a mind, so too does Brahman.

"The original Source, the One, is Brahman's mind, while the entire realm of material existence, added together as a whole, is Its body."

23

"Just as there are different subdivisions, different subdimensions, to material existence, Brahman's body and mind are also constructed of different layers, as are your own.

"These different layers have been referred to in many ways. We will refer to them here as the physical body, the etheric body, the emotional body, the mental body, the astral body, the etheric template, the celestial body, and the causal body.

"Each body and each mind is one degree less material than the last and each one exists within the subdimension that best fits its vibrational signature.

"Beneath all of these layers, at the Source, is Consciousness itself, which has no form whatsoever."

24

"The material world as a whole is therefore the physical form of the living Entity that we refer to as Brahman.

"It is alive and aware, carrying out a life of Its own as It creates and explores and evolves. Just like you.

"All that exists within Its physical body and Its mind are but the individual parts of Its construct."

25

"Just as you have atoms, cells, tissues, and microorganisms living within you, creating and animating your form, and just as each of the individual parts within you is also a living entity, living out a life of its own, so too is it with Brahman.

"This solar system is but one of Its atoms, complete with its own nucleus (the sun) and orbiting electrons (the planets).

"The Milky Way galaxy is but one of Its cells, this universe is but one of Its tissues, and you are as if but a single microorganism living within and off of its vast body."

26

"Life, you see, is a symbiotic relationship between all of the parts and the whole.

"The whole nourishes the parts and gives them life, while the parts contribute to the structure and function of the whole."

27

"All motion within this realm is therefore the motion of Brahman's massive physical presence.

"All events and happenings are but the processes of Its physical form carrying out its tasks.

"As Its 'atoms' (solar systems), 'cells' (galaxies), and 'tissues' (universes) course, existence expands and contracts. Planets spin, stars drift, galaxies whirl, and universes evolve."

28

"Have you not noticed that life on the whole tends to go through 'moods'? Times of abundance and times of scarcity? Times of intolerance and times where tolerance is encouraged? Times when the world seems to be irritable, at war, and times when the world is at relative peace?

"These moods are, likewise, but the mental phases of the universe's own ego mind.

"We are all but the individual parts of Brahman's body and mind that are living out the one life that is Brahma's life, yet Brahman is also, somehow, inexplicably, the summation of all the experiences and moods of our own lives added together.

"All is One. All is interconnected."

29

"One-fourth of Brahman exists within the material world, *as the material world*: as each of its individual parts, as well as the whole.

"This one-fourth of Brahman is that aspect of Its essence that is split into the male and the female, the yang and the yin. The other three-quarters remain within Its Mind, outside the boundaries of physical existence.

"The same occurs with you."

30

"One-fourth of your being is physical, visible. The remainder resides outside the boundaries of physical existence, within the realm of Mind, within the realm of the great Mind, which many refer to as God or Heaven.

"Your attention should be divided in like proportions; one-fourth going to the needs of this material world, with the remaining three-quarters focused on discovering the deepest level of your mind, which is part of, continuous with, and one with the great mind of Brahman.

"The only part of your mind that is separate from the original mind of Brahman is your ego."

31

"Allow me to summarize:

"In the beginning, as I have said, there was nothing but the One; Potential Energy, Consciousness Itself, Awareness Itself, and nothing more.

"As something cannot be created from nothing, physical life must have come from something.

"Since there was nothing other than this One, it stands to reason that physical life was created by It and out of It.

"Thus all physicality is the physical manifestation of the One.

"Brahman is all that you see."

32

"As something cannot come from nothing, the consciousness held within each physical form must have also come from something.

"Since there was nothing other than the One in the beginning, it stands to reason that the consciousness held within the mind of each life form, no matter how large or small, individual or global, was also created by It, and out of It.

"Thus all consciousness is a manifestation, an extension, a continuation of the consciousness of the One.

"Brahman is the One Mind we all share. It is the Collective Consciousness of existence."

33

"Brahman, I hope you now see, is all that exists. It is creation as a whole, as well as each of the individual parts.

"Each part is created out of, and filled with, Brahman's Essence, and each portion participates in the construct and function of the overall whole, which is also a living entity, living out a life of Its own."

34

"The original consciousness of Brahman within each individual part, as well as the whole, remembers what It is and is therefore able to create, explore, experience, and enjoy this world of form without care or angst.

"The lower ego consciousnesses within each individual part, as well as the whole, do not.

"In order to remember, we must all learn how to undergo a great journey into the deepest layers of our minds. We must learn how to transcend our most superficial layers of consciousness in order to discover the deepest, most hidden layers beneath.

"Even the global physical form of Brahman is undergoing this journey of discovery."

"Stop acting so small.
You are the universe in ecstatic motion."

-Rumi

Chapter Two

1

The master thus clarified the powers of the mind to his closest students and began instructing them in the practices that led to their mastery:

2

"Sleep is a process where the outermost layer of the mind—the ego, or waking mind—falls away towards rest and rejuvenation, setting your consciousness free from its daily container.

"With the shackles loosened, your consciousness is able to 'stretch Its legs', so to speak. It is able to wander and explore beyond the limitations and boundaries of waking existence.

"Without this nightly break, without this nightly respite, one would go quite mad, like an animal that has been caged for its entire existence.

"Consciousness does not do well with continual confinement."

3

"The very fact that your consciousness does this—the very fact that it withdraws from the ego, withdraws from the waking mind, and travels, on a nightly basis, into other states of awareness—is proof that such a journey is possible. It is proof that you have the ability.

"For most, though, this journey only occurs by default, during sleep, or with the use of certain drugs. But if you were to study your mind, you may be able to develop a modicum of control over its automated processes.

"Breathing is automated, is it not? Yet you can override its automations and breathe as you wish. The processes of the mind work in a similar fashion, though it is a bit more difficult to tame. You must put forth some effort if you wish to develop the ability."

4

"In your attempt to study, master, and harness the powers of your mind, you must begin by observing it in action, starting with the ego, the most obvious layer.

"Do not attempt to change anything at first, simply observe it. To escape from a prison you must first understand the outlay of the terrain from which you hope to escape.

"Once you understand your ego's machinations, once you understand how it operates, once you understand how its interpretations determine the reality you experience, your escape route will become obvious."

5

"The nature of the ego mind is to wander and to react out of instinct, the instinct to survive. It is trying to protect you.

"If you have chosen to accept its interpretations, you have become its slave. But if you have chosen to fight against its nature, you will have found the struggle to be futile. The ego mind *will* wander; you cannot force it to stop. The ego mind *will* react in the way it has learned to react; you cannot change its reactions. Not directly. You must allow it to be as it is and find another way around.

"'Resist not evil' is the lesson here. The more you resist your ego the more attention you will be placing on it and the stronger its hold over you will become.

"Mastering your ego requires strategy. You must learn to intervene at the right moment, change its machinations gradually, or rise above it. These are the only choices you have at your disposal."

6

"'Stand aside' in your mind and observe, for example, that when someone insults you, your ego mind instinctively suggests that you become angry. According to your ego's way of thinking, having an enemy reduces your chances of survival.

"Without interference, you *will* become angry. Your emotions listen to your ego and your body listens to your emotions. Unless you intervene, your emotions and your body will follow your ego's interpretation. Your face will flush, your breath will catch, and your heart will pound.

"Conversely, you will find that when someone compliments you, your ego instinctively tends to respond in a positive manner. It believes that forming alliances increases your chances of survival. You therefore tend to experience welcomed emotions and pleasant bodily sensations when you receive a compliment.

"Your emotional mind believes whatever it is told, whether it is you who are telling it what to believe or your ego."

7

"By understanding this process, by understanding how the ego works, you may begin to consciously intervene.

"It takes effort, especially in the beginning, but you may decide not to accept your ego's interpretation of an event and, instead, create and insert your own.

"You may decide that a simple insult from a classmate or workmate does not constitute a true threat to your survival. You may therefore *decide* (something the ego cannot do) to interpret the insult as a compliment—the insulter must be jealous. Or you may *decide* to divert your attention onto something else—perhaps a new goal that you are close to reaching.

"Either way, you will have learned how to consciously alter the automated chain of reactions. You will have learned how to bypass the instinctive reactions of your ego and decide for yourself how you wish to react.

"With persistence, practiced enough times, your choice of reactions will, over time, become your ego's default reaction. It will take note of your preferred responses, the lack of a catastrophe when using them, and then follow suit. It will eventually realize that simple insults are not as serious an issue as it took them to be and will therefore learn to interpret them in the manner you have demonstrated.

"As simple and subtle as this practice may seem, it denotes great progress in your journey towards mastery. It allows you to become the 'driver' of your life, so to speak, no longer the witless passenger; no longer a slave to your ego's instinctive interpretations of events.

"You have now learned the first two methods of mastering your ego: how to intervene at the right moment and how to gradually alter its reactions. The last level available to you is to rise above the ego altogether. We will go into this method now."

8

"As you progress with this practice, it may begin to occur to you that there *must* exist an aspect of your mind that is separate from your ego mind; an aspect that is able to *stand outside the ego* and watch as it perceives and interprets the events of your life; an aspect that watches, unattached, as your ego's interpretations ebb and flow back and forth from one dualistic extreme of emotion to another. In short, it may begin to dawn on you that another level of mind *has* to exist for you have now experienced It for yourself.

"With this discovery, you may decide *not* to intervene. You may decide *not* to supersede your ego's interpretations, divert your attention elsewhere, or attempt to train it towards a preferred response. You may choose instead to remain within the vantage point of this other, separate aspect of your mind and simply observe, unattached and unconcerned, as the ego churns away.

"Master this practice, and you will have mastered the third, final, and most important method of dealing with your ego: rising above it.

"As subtle as this may seem, this ability marks another milestone in your progress. Master it and you will have found your way beyond your ego, the lowest level of consciousness within your mind, and into the vantage point of your higher Mind, which is no easy feat."

9

"The next step is to *realize* the magnitude of your achievement. *You have left the ego and entered the higher Mind. You have entered Atman. You have entered Brahman, the Collective Consciousness of existence.*

"Because the accomplishment is subtle, because of the lack of fireworks or some other grandiose indication of attainment, the implications of your success can easily be missed.

"As your awareness of the higher Mind grows, Its presence will become less and less subtle. If you do not take this last step though, if you do not come to *realize* the implications of your success, if you do not come to *realize* the magnitude of your feat, you will miss the opportunity to isolate this aspect of your mind, explore It, and increase your awareness of It.

"Enlightenment is simple and extremely subtle, which I cannot emphasize enough. If you expect it to be complex and blatant, you will miss it."

10

"Sleep, as I previously alluded to, is another event that allows you the chance to practice following your consciousness beyond the waking state and into others. It is another example of rising above, or moving beyond, the confines of the ego.

"The migration of your consciousness during sleep occurs naturally, regularly, involuntarily, so you know it is possible. You know your mind is up to the task. We now want to learn how to consciously reproduce the act while attempting to retain a modicum of control."

11

"Begin by observing the events that lead to sleep and then copy the ritual: Get comfortable in a dark, quiet area, remaining as still as possible. Breathe deeply but slowly, all the while holding on softly, gently, to your awareness.

"With enough practice, you may find yourself able to successfully emulate the ritual. You may develop the ability to 'trick' your surface mind towards slumber, at will, all the while retaining some degree of awareness. This will allow you to remain somewhat alert as your consciousness leaves the vault of the ego, the vault of the waking mind, and into the deeper states of awareness.

"This ritual is also the basis of meditation. The idea is to mimic the dynamics of falling asleep, to push the waking mind towards dormancy, but without losing awareness completely. This is why most prefer to sit during meditation. It is more difficult to lose control of your consciousness when you are sitting. If you do, you will slump or fall over.

"When you were a child, did you ever feign sleep until you were sure your parents had drifted off then sneak out of bed or even the house? What I am describing is similar. The bed or house is the waking mind, the parents are its guards, the ego and you are Consciousness Itself, longing to explore."

12

"The practice of parallelling the process of sleep while retaining a degree of awareness is easier to perform, especially in the beginning, after awakening during the night or first thing in the morning. Half asleep, it is easier to lull your waking mind back towards inactivity while retaining a small degree of awareness.

"Even better is to develop the habit of asking yourself if you are dreaming any time bizarre events occur. Eventually, you will ask this question of yourself while you *are* asleep. When this occurs, focus on your hands. This will solidify the ever-changing landscape of the dream world. Then you may begin to explore.

"Any time you begin to lose awareness, any time the dream world begins to tilt and twirl and change—and it will—concentrate on your hands. This will anchor your consciousness to the dreamscape that you are currently experiencing.

"The practice of retaining consciousness during sleep has been referred to as 'lucid dreaming'."

13

"Dreams are your ego mind's attempts at explaining your experiences while in the dreaming realms. Retain even a small degree of consciousness as you enter these realms, or find a way to gain awareness once you are within them, and these journeys will begin to take on a life of their own.

"The more often you practice the more control you will develop. It will become habitual. You will have your waking life and you will have other lives that you live while within the other realms.

"Do note, though, that it is common to lose consciousness temporarily, right after your ego mind begins to drift, so do not despair. The more intent you are on remaining conscious, the more it is on your mind, the more often you think of it, the more regularly the idea will occur to you, even while within the dreaming realms. This remembrance will become your alert signal that it is time to regain awareness.

"The first time or two you awaken within your dreams you may become alarmed. This is normal and to be expected. You are doing something extraordinary—something you did not know was possible. It will most likely frighten you and you will lose your grip on the dream world. After a few attempts, the alarm will abate.

"Once you can lucid dream without fear, you may still become excited. You may struggle rigorously to hold on to your awareness. This too will cause you to lose your grip on the dream world. Your attempt must be gentle. You must 'fly under the radar' of your waking mind. Remain as calm as possible."

14

"The more you study your mind and how it operates the more successful you will become in being able to copy, emulate, and manipulate its processes.

"Study and practice long enough and you will begin to develop a feel for your consciousness. You will begin to develop the ability to separate Its subtle presence from all else, whenever you wish, and guide it into these other states, these other realms."

15

"There are three main stages of sleep and three corresponding states that are experienced during meditation. Each stage or state is experienced during the migration of your awareness into a different level of consciousness.

"These three stages include light sleep (or the initial meditative state), REM sleep (or the intermediate state of meditation, which is deeper), and non-REM sleep (the deepest stage of sleep and the deepest state of meditation)."

16

"Light sleep is the domain of the first subdimension of consciousness. It is the initial stage of sleep and the initial state of meditation. Here, the ego is still present but struggling to maintain its hold, struggling to remain the filter through which you understand your experiences.

"This subdimension is the one that is most like our own, at least compared to the deeper levels to come. It is but a single degree less dualistic, a single degree less material, than the waking world we are used to. Light sleepers spend a lot of time in this stage. As one ages, one tends to sleep less and less deeply, for reasons I will go over shortly.

"It is common to enter this stage without realizing it. It feels as if you are still awake, imagining different scenarios in your mind. Yet, if you were to say, 'I cannot sleep,' someone near you might say that you *have* been sleeping for they heard you snoring.

"This state is the easiest to reach, the easiest to retain awareness while within, and also the easiest to misconstrue as part of the waking state. Again, it may feel as if you are simply daydreaming. With practice, you will learn to recognize when your mind has made this extremely subtle shift in consciousness.

"Once you realize that you have entered this state, look around. Do not lose yourself to the experience. Remain aware, or regain awareness if you have lost it, and explore."

17

"The stages and states I speak of apply not only to sleep and meditation but also to the imagination. Rational intelligence is bound to the realm of physical reality. Imagination springs into the waking mind from the realms beyond. When you use your imagination, you have discovered yet another route beyond the ego level of the mind and into the deeper states of consciousness.

"Have you not ever troubled yourself with a problem only to have the solution pop effortlessly into your mind once you have given up?

"Have you not ever dreamed of a solution to an issue you could not solve? Of course you have. The greatest minds in society—the seers, scientists, poets, and artists of all ages—have noted this phenomenon well and praised it relentlessly. They claim that all major solutions, all major advancements, all new ideas spring from this unseen source. They emerge not from the realms of what is but from the realms of what could be.

"For most people, these more imaginative solutions only enter our awareness once our rational waking minds have been exhausted; then and only then do the more imaginative solutions surface. As you progress in practice, you will learn how to tap into these states at will, as have the seers, scientists, poets, and artists that I previously mentioned.

"Once again, realization is of utmost importance here. It is only when you *realize* that dreaming, meditating, or diving into your imagination takes you into other realms or states of consciousness that your experiences within them will begin to take on a deeper, more spiritual meaning.

"If you do not realize this, the significance of such experiences will remain lost on you. You will continue to find them commonplace. You will continue to miss the magnitude of what you have experienced."

18

"REM sleep, the intermediate stage of sleep, the intermediate state of meditation, the intermediate territory of the imagination, is the domain of the deeper, more intermediate levels or subdivisions of consciousness. It is experienced when your awareness drifts beyond the initial stage of consciousness, beyond the initial subdimension of awareness, and into the intermediate layers of the mind.

"The ego is still present at this point. It is still holding on, but barely. The waking mind does not fall away all at once. It does so in degrees; thus the existence of stages. The deeper the stage of sleep (or meditation, or imagination) you enter the more the ego, the more the waking mind falters and falls away and the deeper your consciousness is allowed to travel.

"In this stage, we still experience separation and individuality. This is because the intermediate states of the mind retain some degree of duality. The further your consciousness descends the deeper the layers of reality that are reached, the more separation and individuality fade into non-existence. This is why your dreams, your ego's attempts at explanation, your ego's attempts at interpretation, become increasingly bizarre the deeper your consciousness travels. The ego mind is best suited to the world of duality. It cannot logically interpret experiences obtained in the deeper, more unified states of consciousness.

"This also explains why dreams (and meditative experiences and some of your imaginative wanderings) are often prophetic. As your consciousness descends deeper and deeper, it is not only separation that fades but also time. You may dream of, experience meditative events of, or even imagine past, present, or future occurrences."

19

"Non-REM sleep, the final stage of sleep, the deepest state of meditation, the innermost musings of the imagination, is the domain of Brahman, the domain of the higher Mind.

"The more superficial and intermediate stages of sleep represent the stages of *falling* asleep while the stage of deep sleep, and deep sleep alone, represents the stage of *being* asleep, fully asleep. You are not fully asleep until you reach this level.

"Likewise, you have not reached the full meditative state, or the full imaginative state, until you reach this level. Children reach this level easily, which is why they are so hard to rouse when they sleep or daydream.

"Over time, as the reality of the material world becomes more and more ingrained into our psyches, we find it more and more difficult to enter the deepest state of consciousness. This goes for sleep (we become lighter sleepers), meditation, and even the use of imagination.

"Most major discoveries are made by scientists before they reach the age of thirty-three. This is why. We gradually lose our ability to enter the deeper realms of imagination as we age. Our egos have obtained a tighter and tighter grasp on our perception of reality and therefore become increasingly difficult to 'shake'."

20

"The deepest stage of sleep, meditation, and imagination is reached only when the ego or waking mind has been forced to let go completely. We lose ourselves to the experience. We *become* the experience. The reins that had previously held our consciousness in check have finally completed the process of letting go, allowing it to cross over the final barrier.

"The realm it enters is not a subdivision of reality. The realm it enters contains no duality. The realm it enters contains no physicality. The realm it enters is a completely separate dimension.

"This realm is commonly referred to as Heaven or Nirvana."

21

"Do you understand the full measure of what I just said? Each and every night, your consciousness returns home to Brahman! Each and every night, your consciousness returns home to Heaven!

"It does the same during the deepest state of meditation and the deepest state of imaginative exploration.

"These deepest experiences are not usually recollected upon returning to the waking mind for the ego was not present during these experiences, thus the absence of rapid eye movement (REM) while within this level. The ego and the body have let go completely.

"To retain a sense of these experiences, one must learn how to consciously cross the final barrier and retain this level of consciousness once one returns to the waking state, which will eventually occur if you master the practice of lucid dreaming, if you master the science of meditation, if you master the full power and scope of your imagination."

22

"In the beginning stages of practice, the student is encouraged to explore the intermediate states of reality, for conscious experiences within these states indicate progress.

"Eventually though, the master will demand the student let go of even these experiences, for if the student becomes obsessed with the intermediate states, they will not progress to the final stage."*

*This is why Zen masters often carry a stick while observing their students in the meditation room. When the higher level students get caught up in the intermediate states of meditation, the Zen master gives them a whack on the back and orders them to "Let it go." Eventually, you must let even these experiences go in order to allow your attention to continue to expand.

Sufi masters do similarly. They say that fascination with the intermediate realms is normal and to be expected, but after a while they become the new obstacle in your final quest to obtain awareness of the One.

How do you know when you have obtained the One? For one thing, fascination will be replaced with an unshakeable sense of peace.

23

"The innermost Mind, the non-dualistic Mind, the higher Mind, the Collective Consciousness of existence, is the original Mind of Brahman. It has always existed and It always will.

"The lower, outermost layer of the mind—that which we refer to as the waking mind, or ego—is temporary; it is an extension of the higher Mind. It is the outer layer of the original Mind, which was forced to adapt to this world of form when It came into contact with and experienced matter. It is the aspect of your mind that discovered, through trial and error, that you should not pick up snakes, talk to strangers, or jump off cliffs."

24

"Once these lessons have been learned, and the chances of survival have been relatively assured, this lowest level of the mind becomes an impediment to progress for it blocks out the presence of the states of consciousness that exist beneath it.

"This state of mind, the lowest state, in short, represents your Original Consciousness' ability to adapt to whatever environment It finds itself within. It is only necessary while you are here, in this realm, in bodily form. Once you leave this realm, it is no longer needed and so dissipates."

25

"The struggle to rediscover the higher Mind is the ultimate duty and purpose of human life, and a struggle it is.

"The lower ego mind's job is to keep you safe in the realm of physicality, and it does its job well. It demands, at all times, that you remain focused on the task it has been given and stubbornly insists that you pay attention to its perceptions and instructions.

"As it is only aware of that which the external senses have the ability to perceive, it is only aware of itself, and the forms, attributes, and qualities of material existence.

"The higher Mind is entirely ethereal and hidden behind the curtain of the ego mind. It has no form, attributes, or qualities and so remains invisible to the ego.

"The lower mind, through its trials and tribulations with life, has taken over and forgotten its original and deeper essence. As it demands your full attention, it un-wittingly blocks your perception of the deeper corridors that exist within your mind."

26

"Those of us who have experienced Atman, those of us who have experienced Brahman, those of us who have experienced the higher Mind, have come to refer to It, whatever It truly is, as *'neti, neti'* ... 'not this, not that'.

"If your worldly senses can perceive it, if your ego mind can understand it, it is simply not Atman."

27

"Atman, and by extension Brahman, can only be perceived through the development and use of a deeper sense. One that is not of this world. One that surpasses the limitations of waking consciousness and ego interpretation.

"To find Brahman, one must find a way to traverse beyond the level of consciousness that is known as the waking state and wade into those states that exist just beyond.

"I have given you a few methods for doing this: (1) the method of 'standing aside' in your mind, (2) the method of mimicking the process of sleep while retaining awareness, and (3) the process of using your imagination. Now I will go into others.

"Keep in mind, though, that these lessons must be practiced in order for you to progress. Knowledge of them is not enough. Many, during the initial stages of progress, enjoy learning of spiritual practices in order to impress their friends. This is natural and it does represent the initial stages of a growing spiritual longing. But it is not until such methods are actually practiced in earnest that you will truly begin your journey."

28

"Ultimately, we all already have some sense of our higher Mind at work. We all have some sense of Atman, we all have some sense of Brahman, the Collective Consciousness of existence, but most of us do not realize that we do.

"Have you not noticed that trends come and go in waves? If one person comes up with a new idea, several more tend to have come up with the same idea, or one that is similar, at the same time, even though they were separated from each other.

"Have you ever thought about someone you had not seen or heard from in a long time and then they contacted you or visited?

"These phenomena represent the natural yet unconscious processes (for most of us) of tapping into the Collective Consciousness of existence.

"We therefore *are* aware of the higher Mind's existence, at least to a certain extent. We *are* connected with It and we *do* experience It, but unconsciously so. We become so focused on the manifestations of life, the dramas and dilemmas and outer workings of our individual situations, at the insistence of our egos, that we do not notice Its subtle presence and therefore do not focus on It, study It, or come to know It."

29

"Because the higher Mind's presence is so subtle, and mixed in with all else, we fail to perceive It. In doing so, we fail to realize the magic of life. We fail to acknowledge the underlying Intelligence of existence and focus instead only on that which we can see and hear and taste and feel and smell, which we come to view as routine.

"We forget to ask by what Intelligence it is that the things we see and hear and taste and feel and smell are able to exist.

"We forget to ask by what Power it is that we have the ability to see and hear and taste and feel and smell them.

"We forget to ask by what Intelligence it is that we have consciousness and so miss the miracle. It does not enter into our awareness even though It is right here, right now, within us and all around us."

30

"Because Brahman's presence is so indistinct, so faint, we tend to focus not on It but on the distractions of the ego and the tribulations of material existence, which are anything but subtle.

"We do feel Brahman, we do sense It, but we do not know that we do. We do not know how to separate our awareness of It from the feelings that we obtain from the world of form around us, so we transfer our love and longing for It to that which we *are* able to see and hear and taste and feel and smell.

"These things *seem* to be the source of our love, the source of our longings, for they contain It. But they are not It. Not fully. All that you can sense with the five senses is a fraction of the Whole, but we desire the Whole. We desire the Unity.

"All feelings of love, in the end, are the feelings of love we have for Atman-Brahman.

"All desires, all longings, all needs, all curiosities are, in the end, the single desire, the single longing, the single need, the single curiosity we have for Atman-Brahman."

31

"Most do not realize it, but we do not love and connect with a person; we love and connect with the Soul of that person.

"We do not love and connect with dogs or cats, flowers or sunsets; we love and connect with That which creates and animates dogs and cats, flowers and sunsets. We love and connect with the Essence of these things. We love and connect with the consciousness of these things. We love and connect with the Intelligence that governs these things. We love and connect with the Life that is held within these things. We love and connect with the Soul of these things.

"We *already* experience Brahman. We *already* have That which we seek. Once again, I must remind you that the journey towards enlightenment is actually the journey towards realization. The shift in understanding that leads to enlightenment is incredibly subtle, yet its acquisition changes everything."

32

"The true Object of our desires, the true Object of our longings, the true Object of our needs, the true Object of our curiosity is obscured by the ego, our lowest level of consciousness, and its dependence on the senses.

"The ego therefore mistakenly seeks the love of Brahman within the world of form. Thus is the desire for riches and power, fame and control, and all other worldy boons created.

"We think that we can obtain safety, we think that we can obtain survival, love, and comfort through the procurement of such things, but we cannot.

"They hint at That which we seek, for we feel It within them, but they do not deliver. They cannot. This is why they are all, ultimately, unfulfilling."

33

"Even the insatiable desire for sex is nothing but the longing of the dualistic male and female energies to merge back into the One. But even sex does not deliver. Not completely.

"During sex, the two participants merge for a moment, during which they lose themselves in the moment, during which they enter into the Now, during which they move beyond the consciousness of waking duality and, for a time, experience the higher, more unified state of ecstasy.

"But once the act is over, the connection is lost."*

*What about those who are attracted to members of their same gender? According to Upanishadic and ancient Egyptian concepts, the same Law of Attraction still applies...

Homosexuals are simply those that have been born with a hormonal configuration that gives them the bodily presentation of a male or female, but as they grow and mature, as their hormone system evolves, the configuration becomes altered, or flipped, to a greater or lesser degree. They still portray the outer sexual characteristics of their gender but may begin to take on the hormonal configuration, along with the preferences, and even some of the mannerisms, of the other.

A female, for example, that develops a more yang (testosterone-dominant) configuration of hormones as they *reach maturity may be drawn to the opposing yin (estrogen-dominant) configuration of other females. A male that develops a more yin presentation may likewise be drawn to the opposing yang energy of other males.*

What about those who are attracted to both sexes? Their hormonal charge is dynamically neutral. It fluctuates between yang and yin and therefore so do their interests.

What about those who do not enjoy sex and never have? Their hormonal configuration is statically neutral. Once they reach maturity, they have no dominant expression of hormones and therefore have no opposing expression to crave.

34

"Finding Brahman is actually easy. It is the most natural thing in the world to accomplish. But most seek It as something grandiose, as something spectacular and loud and obvious, as something that is far away and separate from their own being. This is why they miss It.

"It is not 'out there' somewhere. It is not something you need to travel far and wide to find. It is not something you need to read your entire life to discover. It is not even something you need to strive for. *It is, instead, the closest most intimate aspect of your own being. It is your own sense of self, your own feeling of home.*

"To find Brahman, you need only to discover, explore, and develop a relationship with your Self."

35

"Without leaving your room you can find It. Without taking a single step, you can discover It. Without looking out of a window, you can realize it. Without reading a single book, you can experience It.

"Its presence is not something you need to search for but something you need to become sensitive to; something you must learn to focus your attention on despite the overwhelming outward distractions of physical existence.

"You must learn how to direct your attention inward. You must learn how to experience and explore your own beingness."

36

"How subtle is Brahman? It is as subtle as love.

"Have you not ever felt love? Of course you have. Yet you found It too simple to be the answer.

"Do you not have consciousness? Of course you do, but you take it for granted. You do not focus on it. You do not explore It. You do not study it. You do not ponder its source. You live your life unconsciously, by default, focused on external phenomena, unaware that you are aware, oblivious to your own sacred presence.

"You cast Love and Consciousness aside and look elsewhere for Brahman, yet finding Brahman is as easy as realizing that It *is* your own feeling of self, realizing that It *is* your own sense of home, and focusing on feeling Its subtle presence within you, above all else.

"Focus on It and your sense of It will grow."

37

"You already have That which you are seeking. You already *are* That which you are seeking. You take It with you wherever you go.

"Once you realize this, never let the realization go, no matter the storms that rage about you.

"If you choose to remain within your own Center, if you choose to remain within your own Being, if you choose to identify with It (instead of your ego), no matter what transpires you will remain safe. You will hardly even notice the storms.

"Leave Its center, though, and the storms of life will consume you."

38

"Realization of the one true Object of all love, realization of the one true Object of all desire, realization of the one true Object of all longing, realization of the one true Object of all need, realization of the one true Object of all curiosity leads to the realization of the deepest layer of your Mind; the realization of Atman, and by extension the realization of Brahman.

"It is already here, waiting to be noticed. Let go of the constant chatter of your ego mind and focus on Its subtle presence within you, above all else, and you will find It. All suffering will vanish and you will know only peace and comfort.

"Only to the one whose mind is still does the realization of Atman-Brahman begin to emerge."

39

"Quieting the mind is difficult, yet the incessant babbling of your ego is the glue out of which your current level of perception is held together. The trick is not to attempt to subdue it but to ignore it, to let it do as it is designed to do, but pay it no mind, unless or until it is needed. This is how you calm your mind.

"Let go of your internal ramblings, cease losing yourself to them, quit defining yourself by them, and your ego will fade from your awareness. Your higher Mind will take over and the limitations of reality as you now know them will fall apart.

"The transition will be subtle, though, as I keep reminding you. You will have to work at it, but Its presence will grow within your awareness if you find a way to focus on It."

40

"In order to calm your mind, you must also let go of the past and cease living for the future. These are also distractions of the ego.

"The original mind of Brahman, the higher Mind, operates only in the Now. That is where you will find It."

41

"Like calming the mind, living in the present can also be difficult.

"The ego cannot survive in the present. As it does not wish to be set aside, it jealously guards against the discovery of the Now with constant distractions, projecting memories of the past (yang) and musings of the future (yin) over the present moment like a veil.

"Right now, I can assure you that you do not experience the present moment as it really is. All that you currently experience is your ego's interpretation of present events as they are viewed through the mirror of past experiences and the telescope of future hopes and anxieties. Step outside the filter of the ego and a new perception of what lies before you will emerge.

"Will that new perception be subtle? Yes, it will. At least at first. I know I keep repeating myself, but this is very important. It is the linchpin to success.

"When you learned the truth about Santa Claus, your entire perception of the world changed, did it not? Yet at the same time, nothing changed. All remained as it ever was, yet you instantly viewed it differently.

"Enlightenment is the same. The world will stay the same, but your perception of it will change; subtly at first, then more dramatically over time."

42

"Whenever you observe the Now, whenever you truly live in the moment, you *have* moved your consciousness from the dualistic level of your ego and into the unified vantage point of your higher Mind.

"As subtle, simple, and easy as this may sound, it is the truth. When your consciousness touches the present moment, you touch Brahman. Realize this and life will begin to take on a new meaning."

43

"If you are able to do this, if you are able to let go of the ramblings of your ego mind, if you are able to remember to live in the present and only in the present, if you can remember to retain your feeling of self at all times, the storms of life will subside. What in the world is wrong with this moment if you do not think about it?

"Cast your ego aside and you will find that there is nothing wrong with this moment. It is exactly as it is meant to be. *You* are exactly as you are meant to be."

44

"You already have it all. Nothing is separate from you. Nothing has been kept from you.

"The illusion of separation, the illusion of lack, the illusion of need, dissolves when you find that sense of self and home within you, for then you come to realize that you already have all that you have ever wanted and more. You come to realize that you *are* all that you have ever wanted and more.

"YOU are the treasure that you have been seeking."

45

"All that exists, I hope you now see, is One. All that is, was, or ever will be is created from, and resides within, the single, continuous thread of the Energy, born of Consciousness, that we summarize as Brahman.

"All plants, animals, and humans—all living beings— are as if but a single wandering Soul that is lost in a dream of Its own creation, oblivious to Its connection with each other and the Cosmic Soul."

46

"Within the interconnected web of Energy that forms the material world all beings live, act, and interact with 'the Field'.

"'The Field' affects all the individual players within it, and the actions of each individual actor, in turn, affect all the other actors as well as 'the Field' Itself.

"We all live symbiotically. The moods and actions of 'the Field', and the moods and actions of the actors within It, produce the fruit that we all separately and cumulatively experience together."

47

"If a butterfly was to flap its wings in Tokyo, for example, it could change the weather in Hungary.

"If a person was to steal from another, its effects would be felt throughout the rest of 'the Field'.

"If a person was to perform a good, kind, and selfless act, the results would likewise reverberate throughout the whole of existence, like a small ripple traversing a great pond.

"If an atom was to be split on one side of this universe, atoms found on the far side would be affected. Even atoms found in other universes, in other subdimensions, would be affected.

"If 'the Field' were to cease expanding and begin to contract, it would likewise affect each individual form of life within it, on both the physical and emotional level.

"This occurs because all is One. All is interconnected within the vast web of Energy, Consciousness, Intelligence, or Love that we refer to as Brahman."

48

"I have referred to Atman as the individual Soul and Brahman as the All-Soul. This may give you the idea that there are many Souls.

"There are not. There is but one Soul, as I just alluded to. Did you catch it? I said, 'All plants, animals, and humans—all living beings—are as if but a *single* wandering Soul that is lost in a dream of Its own creation, oblivious to Its connection with each other and the Cosmic Soul.'

"We are all but extensions, continuations of this Cosmic Soul, whatever It truly is. It is us and we are It.

"This one Soul is creating, exploring, and experiencing life within a myriad of forms, both individual and global, and even within a myriad of subdimensions. It may be wearing different outward disguises, and It may be expressing itself through different personalities we refer to as egos, but It is, I can assure you, the same exact Soul that is residing within each of us and life as a whole."

49

"In a way, life is very much like the quaking aspen tree. Entire colonies of this tree, even entire groves of this tree, grow out of a single, shared system of roots, all of which emanate from, and connect to, a common central root.

"Each tree is given life by the same root, nourished by the same root, and connected to all others at this root.

"Each tree is alive, living out a life of its own, yet each tree is also living out the one life of the one root and all that exists within its network. When one tree dies, another springs up from the common root.

"Each individual tree may look different, and each individual tree may have its own idiosyncrasies, but only on the surface, for each tree is nothing but a continuation, an above-ground expression, of the same central root, which lies hidden below the surface.

"As with our lives, this connection is not readily apparent. One must explore below the surface to find it."

50

"We are all one. You are everywhere. You are everything. You are a continuation of the single mysterious Root of Life that we refer to as Brahman."

"Split a piece of wood, and I am there.
Lift up a rock, and you will find me
there."

-Jesus; the Gospel of Thomas, 77b.

Chapter Three

1

Ten ancient sages continued the discussion on
the nature of reality:

2

"Imagine Brahman as a great tree—the Tree of Life.

"The above-ground aspects of the tree—the trunk, the branches, the leaves, and the fruit—represent the Universal Body of Brahman, the physical aspects of life; that which is most easily and readily perceived.

"The root system and the soil beneath represent the hidden source of the tree's existence.

"Thus are there two main realms: the realm above and the realm below.

"The aspects of the tree, and life in general, that are obvious are only made possible by the aspects of the tree, the aspects of life, that are not."

3

"In order to simplify matters, we often speak of and study these two aspects—the visible and the hidden—separately, but they are not.

"The above-ground representations of the tree are but an extension, a continuation, an outgrowth, of That which lies beneath."

4

"In the timeless beginning, there was the soil, and only the soil; rich in sustenance, rich in potential.

"This soil is the veritable Soup of Creation; That which we refer to as Heaven, the One, the Source.

"The soil's nature is to nourish, to create, to give life— and so it did. A seed was formed.

"This seed was Atman."*

*Atman is the name Hindus use when they refer to the individual Soul ("the seed"), which arose from the All-Soul ("the soil").

Note how similar the term Atman is to the more modern renderings of the same concept: Adam, for example, is the Christian version, the first manifestation of physical life. Atum is the Egyptian version, and atom is modern science's rendering.

I will go deeper into these similarities in my future works on the Upanishads.

5

"Nourished and encouraged by the soil, Atman sprouted from its shell and rooted itself deep within the substrate below. Then It began to reach up towards the realm above.

"Both the root system of the tree, which resides just below the surface, and the trunk, which extends far above it, represent Atman.

"Atman therefore lives a dual reality. It is part of the world below but also part of the world above. It marks the transition point between the two realms. It is what anchors physical existence, and all within it, to the nutrient-dense soil of Heaven."

*In the previous chapter's scenario, which used the quaking aspen tree as an example, the root was symbolized as Brahman. In this scenario, the soil represents Brahman while Atman represents the root system. Otherwise, the two scenarios remain consistent.

This scenario represents an expansion of the previous scenario.

6

"The main branches of the tree grow out of the trunk, out of Atman, and represent the subdimensions of above-ground life. Each one represents a different subreality, a different substratum.

"The intermediate branches of the tree grow out of the main branches. They represent the collateral realms that branch off the main subdimensions of above-ground life. Within Brahman's house there are many rooms, many realms, many divisions.

"The smallest branches, the terminal branches, sprout out from the intermediate branches and represent the species of life found within each subdimension.

"The leaves represent the individual life forms within each subdimension, while the fruit represents those evolved souls that have blossomed into a higher state of expression and awareness."

7

"The fruit is the ultimate product of the tree, the entire purpose of the tree, and the culmination of Its efforts. They are the reason the tree was inspired to form.

"The fruit holds the seeds out of which other trees are born and driven to produce fruit of their own.

"Existence has known not one life but many. From each cycle of existence emerges the next."

*A scientist has now found that there has not been one Big Bang but many. Each universe that exists was born out of a previous black hole and will eventually be absorbed back into a black hole of its own. A new Big Bang will then emerge from the last, creating a new universe, like a phoenix rising from the ashes.

Scientists have also discovered light emerging from beyond black holes, intimating the existence of life on the other side. Perhaps it is from this life beyond that these new universes emerge.

8

"This growth, this profusion, this expansion, did not occur all at once and then cease. It is continuing, even now, at this very moment.

"The current Tree of Life is expanding, maturing, budding branches, subbranches, collaterals, terminal branches, and leaves, as well as the fruit out of which new trees will be produced.

"Each and every seed from each and every fruit contains the DNA, the Essence, the germ of the soil.

"As one tree dies, another is born from the seed of Its previous incarnation, always containing the same original genetic essence of the One, the same nutritive substrate of the soil."

9

"Notice the structural outlay of the tree:

"There are many leaves on the tree, fewer terminal branches, even fewer intermediate branches, and still fewer main branches. Yet there is a single trunk and a single root bulb.

"This represents the structural outlay of the Soul's expression. The more outward Its expression the more individualistic and multitudinous It becomes. The more centralized Its expression the more unified.

"Ponder this for a moment."

10

"Each and every aspect of the tree is alive, living out a life of its own, yet each aspect is also part of a greater whole, part of a greater life, part of a greater purpose.

"Most of us have become so focused on our individual life as a 'leaf' that we have forgotten that the Tree of Life is actually a single entity."

11

"Which parts of the tree survive death? Is this not what you really desire to know?

"Each and every part of the tree survives death, in one way or another, for each and every part is recycled into new life. When the tree dies, or a part of the tree dies, it simply falls to the earth and erodes back into the soil.

"What you are really asking is whether or not *your consciousness* will survive death. Is this not so? Whether or not it will remain intact. Whether or not you will still be. Whether or not you will remain aware of your existence.

"The answer is yes, your consciousness does survive death but not in the manner in which you are asking.

"This is the main concept we have come before you to explain."

12

"You now believe yourself to be but a single 'leaf' in the Tree of Life, separate from the rest of the tree, but you are not. You carry within you the same sustenance, the same consciousness, the same DNA, the same underlying Essence, as the rest of the tree, which It obtains from the soil.

"Your deepest level of consciousness, your deepest Essence, does survive death intact. Your most superficial level, however, that which we refer to as the 'leaf', the ego, the consciousness of individual existence, does not. It cannot.

"The ego is not real. It is a byproduct of material existence. It was created out of a combination of inherited preferences, accumulated experiences, and the pressures of family, friends, and society.

"When death comes, it *will* take your ego with it. It will take your current concept of self—your preferences and aversions. But the deepest level of consciousness within you—the consciousness of the tree Itself, the consciousness of the soil, the consciousness of Brahman, the Principle of Life, the Essence of existence—does go on intact."

13

"Do you find this disappointing? Are you upset to discover that your current concept of self, your current identity, does not survive death?

"Most do, but you will find that death is not so much the loss of who and what you now take yourself to be as much as it is the realization that you are far more than you could have ever hoped to imagine.

"You are not, and never have been, a separate entity. You are not, and never have been, alone. You are not, and never have been, a single 'leaf'. You are the very soil out of which the Tree of Life has emerged. You are the nutritional soup that gave birth to the tree and nourishes its existence."

14

"Still, one's individual nature, one's individual idea of oneself, does survive death in a way.

"You *will* remember who and what you previously thought yourself to be, at least at first, but you will not wish to return to that separate identity. Once free of that cage, you will never wish to go back. Once you realize that you are the entire tree, and the soil that created it, you will not miss having the individualized consciousness of a 'leaf'.

"In time, though, you will forget your previous existence, just as your memories of childhood fade more and more in the latter years of life.

"Does this disturb you? If so, why? Does a butterfly or moth mourn the loss of its previous form when it emerges from its cocoon? It does not. Does a parent wish to return to a time before the existence of their children? They do not. Do you wish to return to having the mental maturity of a child? No, you do not.

"Death is similar."

15

"One's actions, one's works, one's contributions also survive death.

"Due to the earthly law of Karma, and the interconnectedness of all things, the footprints of one's life remain and continue to affect the world at large even after the death of the body, the ego, and the earthly senses. But after death, you will no longer take your previous identity, or your previous actions, with you. You will no longer define yourself by them. You will not feel the need to."

16

"When you became an adult, did you continue to identify with your childhood behaviors? Did you wish to remain in the same house, sleep in the same bed, play with the same toys, and act in the same manner? No, you did not.

"You entered a new chapter of your life, complete with a new outlook, a new level of awareness, a new set of goals, and a new set of interests. You let go of the old and eagerly struck out to explore the new.

"Death works in the same manner. It is but a new chapter to your existence; a new level of growth."

17

"Do you have to wait for death to see this? No, you do not.

"Existence is a state of mind. Learn to transcend your current state of mind, learn to transcend your ego's point of view, and you will experience the Essence of your being.

"Practice long enough and you will discover your own Essence to be the common sap that runs through us all."

18

"There may be many leaves on the Tree of Life and there may be many branches, but all the leaves and branches emanate from the same trunk, the same root ball, the same soil.

"You, I, and all that exist, when broken down into our basest elements, are nothing but unique configurations of the nutrients of the soil. We may have been given different shapes, sizes, and densities, but in the end, we *are* the nutrient-dense substrate of the soil."

19

"Is the process of discovering this truth difficult? Yes, but it is possible, as is evidenced by the fact that many have done so before. Those that have are the Hermeses, Krishnas, Buddhas, Jesuses, Muhammeds, and Bahá'u'lláhs of this world, just to name a few.

"These seekers were able to develop a 'dual awareness'. They found a way to become aware of their deeper Essence while remaining conscious of their concurrent existence as an individual entity. They developed the ability to live in this realm while obtaining an awareness of their deeper connection.

"They found a way to be 'in this world but not of it.'"

20

"If you are able to transcend your ego, if you are able to transcend your current state of mind, if you are able to let go of your individual identity, all sin and error, evil and selfishness, suffering and disillusionment will fall from you as water falls from the back of a duck. These things are attached to the 'leaf' and only the 'leaf'.

"Only as a 'leaf' do you think and act with selfish regard.

"Only as a 'leaf' do you feel alone, become defensive, and suffer.

"Only as a 'leaf' do you fear death.

"Once you realize the truth, you will begin living for the betterment of *the whole tree*, not just yourself.

"At this point, no one will need to tell you that you should not kill, steal, or harm another. It will become your nature not to do such things. You will have transcended the nature you were given at birth and claimed the nature of Brahman as your own."

21

"When you relinquish identifying with the 'leaf', the elements of the physical world will continue to eat away at it, as will the Karma from your previous actions, but you will no longer be attached. You will remain aware of what is happening to your 'leaf', but when death comes, you will leave it and its Karma behind. You will move on.

"Continue to identify with the 'leaf' though, continue to cling to your ego, and its fate will become your own."

22

"Relinquish your identity as a 'leaf', so to speak, and you will still be expected to contribute to this world, for we all have our roles to perform in the overall play of life. Even enlightenment does not deliver us from this responsibility.

"We are all living out our roles as Brahman, the Intelligence of the soil, dictates, whether we are aware of it or not.

"Become aware of your role, become aware of your connection to the soil, and your role will change. You will take on the task of delivering others from the prison of self-identity."

23

"We all have our roles to play? We all have our place? Even sinners?

"Yes, we all have our roles. Sinners and saints, liberals and conservatives, householders and businessmen alike. All are holy. All are needed. All are doing as Brahman dictates."

24

"'But what could a sinner possibly contribute?' you may ask.

"How about teaching us to love, be patient with, and tolerant of all?

"It is easy to love, be patient with, and tolerant of those who are 'good', those you agree with, those you already like, but you have been commanded to love, be patient with, and tolerant of all, even your 'enemies'.

"Sinners therefore exist to test your ability to live and love unconditionally, and such a one becomes part of your life when the need for that lesson is reached. They are the 'petty tyrants' of your life, and your reaction to them is the barometer by which your progress may be gauged.

"They too will evolve. Even sinners will ripen. Each in their own time, each in their own way. For now, though, this is the role that is expected of them. They are living out the nature that Brahman has endowed them with. Until they mature beyond their inherited instinctive natures, they will not be able to do otherwise.

"You have done the same. You too have been the 'petty tyrant' of many others."

25

"As the soil from which you have come, the soil from which you extract your sustenance, is remembered, your ego will die as a reality. Ignorance, individual preferences, frustrations, and sufferings will finally be seen as products of your own creation.

"It is at this point that you will have been born again. This time into Spirit.

"It is at this point that you will override destiny and begin to live consciously, by free will.

"It is at this point that you will realize the greater role that you are here to perform."

26

"When you are finally ready, when your level of consciousness has finally evolved, ripened, and matured to the point that the material world, individuality, and all of its pleasantries have lost their appeal and your interests begin lying elsewhere, a new reality will seek you out. For every step you take towards It, It will take two towards you.

"Your only remaining prayer at this point will be for deliverance 'from the unreal to the Real, from the darkness to the Light, from the mortal to the Immortal'."

27

"When you reach this point, you will no longer care which way the wind blows.

"When you reach this point, you will no longer care what occurs or does not occur.

"When you reach this point, you will no longer care about the religious affiliation of another, the political persuasion of another or the path of another.

"When you reach this point, even the fear of death will begin to lose its sting, for you will see for yourself that it does not exist; at least not in the way that you had previously imagined. It will become no more than the changing of rooms, the changing of levels of consciousness, within which you explore."

28

"For the one that finds Atman, and by extension Brahman—that feeling of Self, that feeling of home within—and remains within It, there will be no more fear.

"Brahman, the soil, lives from this level of perception and so lives beyond the cares of this world. Even if the Tree itself fell, Brahman would still be. It would simply start over. It would create a new one.

"You can do the same. But in order to do so you must let go, once and for all, of your ego and all previous knowledge.

"You do not discover this level of perception, you see, by learning more but by 'unlearning' all that you have previously come to believe.

"One must therefore let go of all that has been learned from parents, family, friends, teachers, books, and society as a whole."

29

"As of right now, we can assure you that what you are seeing, that what you are experiencing, that what you currently think you know is only that which you have been taught to see, experience, and believe.

"You are not perceiving life as it actually is but only as you have previously learned to perceive it. You are experiencing the present moment through the filter of the ego, which interprets what it sees through the lens of past experiences and future hopes and anxieties.

"There is more to what lies before you and within you than you currently realize."

30

"The ego, your individual identity, fears destruction and so fights with all its might any knowledge that might transcend this world, any knowledge that might transcend its vantage point.

"It thinks that another vantage point would mean the death of its existence. And it does.

"Since you still think you are your ego, since you still think you are but a 'leaf', you accept your ego's fear of death as the fear of your own.

"This is not true. You are far more than your ego. You are far more than what it tells you that you are.

"Observe life with a fresh mind, unclouded by previous experiences, unclouded by previous beliefs, unclouded by previous perceptions, and a different level of experience, a different level of perception, a different concept of self will emerge.

"You will find yourself viewing all that transpires from within a different state of mind.

"This is enlightenment. Nothing really changes, yet at the same time, everything will change for you."

31

"Empty your cup of ego. Empty your cup of all past learnings and all past beliefs so that Atman, so that Brahman can enter and fill it for you anew.

"As long as your cup remains full, as long as you still think you know everything, as long as you still think you are your ego and believe what it is telling you, the true magic of existence will not be able to enter."

32

"Your cup seems to be full, and it is. But what you have filled it with is subjective reality, individual reality, not objective reality.

"You view life only from your own individual point of view. You give it the meaning you wish it to have, based around your own wants, needs, and idiosyncrasies. You have filled your cup to the brim with the limited and subjective perceptions of your ego, crowding out the un-limited and objective perspective of your higher Mind.

"Empty your mind. See all that is as if for the first time, every time, and allow Atman-Brahman to show you a new reality. Do so and you will finally obtain the peace you have craved for so long to obtain.

"In order to do so, in order to find and enter Heaven, in order to find and enter Nirvana, in order to transcend the ego one must become like a small child, open to the wonder and awe of life, not bogged down like an adult with a lifetime of learning."

33

"A child does not yet know all there is to know.

"A child has not yet defined everything or had everything defined for them.

"A child sees what is, as it actually is, unfiltered by its undeveloped ego.

"A child is curious, eager, open to all, as opposed to adults who care only about defending their own ego's opinions, vantage points, and perspectives.

"Observe all that you see, hear, touch, taste, and smell from this moment on with a fresh, unclouded and unsullied mind, as if for the first time every time, and the Kingdom is close at hand.

"Realize that you have given everything you experience the meaning it now has for you, and let go of this meaning, and you will awaken to a world of wonder.

"Add to this regular meditation—simply sitting in stillness and observing the silent spaces between your thoughts—and the Kingdom is closer still."

34

"Where do the thoughts of Atman, the higher Mind, and therefore Brahman, reside?

"They reside in the silent spaces between your lower mind's thoughts. They reside between the constant and not-so-subtle musings, babblings, and internal dialogue of your ego.

"To 'hear' its voice, you must enter the Now, which is not accessible to the ego."

35

"We say 'hear' because you do not 'hear' these thoughts, you feel them—you experience them.

"Enter, experience, and immerse yourself within the silence and you will *become* the silence.

"The experience will be subtle at first, and easy to miss, but with practice, the magnitude of your discovery will emerge. You will eventually realize that you *are* the silence.

"The deeper your realization the deeper your transcendence."

36

"Within you, there is a state of mind that simply watches, unattached and unconcerned, tranquil and at peace, as the storms of life roar on.

"We call this aspect of your being the Watcher, Atman, the Soul."

37

"In order to find, enter, experience, immerse yourself within, and hold on to the silence, move your vantage point from that of your ego and into that of the Watcher within.

"To assume this state of mind, simply observe, without preference, without judgement, all that goes on. Do so and you will have transcended the ego. You will have pulled your consciousness from its lower level of perception and guided it into the perspective of Atman-Brahman, the Watcher within."

38

"Do you understand the full measure of what we just said? When your consciousness is pulled from the level of your ego, you cease being the ego! When you guide your consciousness into the perspective of the Watcher, you become the Watcher! You become Brahman! Or, more to the point, you realize that you always have been, not the ego you now take yourself to be.

"The process is that simple.

"Is it easy? Not in the least. The ego is tenacious. But with practice and persistence, you will be able to hold this perspective for extended periods of time. Eventually, it will become habit; it will become second nature.

"It all boils down to a battle of wills. Is your will stronger than that of your ego? If so, you will prevail.

"We must once again warn, though, that at least in the beginning, the experience will be extremely subtle; its import can easily be missed. The longer you are able to do this the more the realization of what you have accomplished will sink in."

39

"A change in what you focus your attention on is all it takes to discover Atman, and by extension Brahman.

"As of now, you focus almost exclusively on your internal thoughts, your internal dialogue, not the silence spaces between.

"As of now, you focus almost exclusively on the past and the future, almost never the present.

"As of now, you focus almost exclusively on the external world, not your internal home.

"Alter the focus of your attention and you will change your identity and your reality."

40

"In order to bypass your ego identity and find Brahman, you must give up your opinions. You must give up your arguments, your political leanings, your prejudices, your religious preferences, and your attachments to worldly wealth and power.

"You must learn to take on the vantage point of the Watcher within you, which simply observes all that transpires without judgment or preference."

41

"The ego is a state of mind. It is what turns your life into a Heaven or a Hell. Give up your preferences and opinions and you will finally obtain peace."

42

"How do you get rid of your ego? How do you give up your preferences, aversions, and opinions? Not by fighting against them.

"When you fight against these things, you bring them more into focus. You give them more attention. You feed them and allow them to grow. While you are focused on them, nothing else will be able to enter into your awareness.

"This is the secret science of the mind. This is how your mind works. It cannot serve two masters. Whatever it is that you focus your attention on expands, while whatever you do not focus your attention on fades.

"When you experienced your first kiss, did the rest of the world not vanish? Did you not focus so hard on the event that you noticed nothing else? What I am describing is similar.

"To defeat the ego, focus your attention not on it but on the present moment, the silence between your thoughts, the feeling of self and home within you, and the incessant babbling of your ego will fall out of your awareness of its own accord.

"Again, 'resist not evil' is the lesson here."

43

"The more you are able to do this, the more you are able to sense Atman-Brahman, the more there will be to sense. It is a Fountain that can never run dry.

"It is Love, and the more of It you give away the more you will have at your disposal."

44

"This is a great dilemma for humans, for we seem to think that the more of a thing that is hoarded the more of it we will have.

"We therefore demand love—as well as power, status, and wealth—in hopes of increasing our chances of survival and comfort. But love works in the opposite manner.

"The only way to obtain love, the only way to obtain Atman, the only way to obtain Brahman, is to give it away, without condition.

"Work without thought of reward. Give without thought of recompense. Act for the sake of acting. Give for the sake of giving. Love for the sake of loving.

"This is the way beyond ego. This is the way of the Soil. This is the way of Brahman. This is the way *to* Brahman."

45

"Brahman, the Soil, gives to every part of the tree equally. It even feeds the weeds that grow around the tree, stealing nutrients. It even feeds the vines that wrap around the tree, strangling it.

"It does all these things yet It never brags. It does all these things yet It never boasts. It does all these things yet It never asks for a thing in return.

"How different we are from Brahman."

46

"Like merges with like. As a drop of water that comes into contact with the ocean merges back into the ocean, so too is it with your consciousness, your Soul, and the ocean of Soul that is Brahman.

"By acting like Brahman—by loving without condition, by giving without thought of reward—you become like Brahman. By becoming like Brahman, your consciousness merges back into the Collective Consciousness of Brahman.

"It is your ego, and your ego alone, that caused you to think that you were separate. It is your ego, and your ego alone, that has caused you to live a life based around self-interests. It is your ego, and your ego alone, that has caused you to suffer.

"Your ego, in the end, is Satan, the devil on your shoulder, the Great Deceiver that all Holy Works have spoken of."

47

"You are not just a 'leaf' on the Tree of Life. You are an extension of the Soil, an extension of the substrate from which the tree emerged.

"What does this substrate represent? It represents the One, the original mind of Brahman, the Collective Consciousness of existence. It represents the Intelligence that created your form, beats your heart, courses blood through your vessels, and digests your food ... the Intelligence that creates and holds the stars in place, spins the planets and slings them around the sun with unerring precision.

"Can this Intelligence be harmed? Of course not. No blade can reach It, no stone can touch It, no fire can burn It. The mortal vessel through which It flows can be damaged, hindering its outward expression, but the Intelligence within it is invulnerable.

"With the death of your body, you will see this. With the death of your body, you will remain."

48

"Immortality and imperviousness, the very things that you wish for most, are already yours, just not yet realized. Realize them and they are yours.

"You can claim them any time you wish. Why not now?

"Do so and you will finally know the same peace that we have found."

"One day Alice came to a fork in the road and saw a Cheshire cat in a tree. 'Which road do I take?' she asked. 'Where do you want to go?' was his response. 'I don't know,' Alice answered. 'Then,' said the cat, 'it doesn't matter.'"

-Lewis Carroll

Chapter Four

1

Yajnavalka himself conversed with one of his students*:

*If you remember from the introduction, Yajnavalkya is credited with authoring most of the Brihadaranyaka Upanishad. However, scholars believe it is more likely an accumulation of writings from several different contributors.

2

"You still seem to be having trouble with the concept of Atman, and by extension Brahman.

"In order to aid you in your efforts, I feel it would be best to use a modern analogy to show you how Atman, how Brahman, fits into your current world view.

"Once you understand the role It plays, once you understand what It is and what It does, using terms you may be more familiar with, Its presence may become more obvious."

3

"What is it that animates a computer? What is it that brings it to life? Is it the hardware—the central processing unit, the screen, the keyboard, the mouse? No, it is not.

"Without an energy source, these things are worthless. Without an energy source, they can do nothing. Without an energy source, they are but wires encased within metal and plastic.

"Plug the computer into an electrical outlet, though, and all this changes.

"It is the same with your body."

4

"But does the body not create its own energy, its own electricity? Does it not have mitochondria and nerve cells that act as generators and conductors?

"Once it has been given life, yes, these generators kick in, but what is the source of energy that gives them that initial spark? What is the source of energy that brings the body's own generators to life?"

5

"If energy is what animates the computer, then what is it that tells the computer what to do, how to do it, and when? Is it the central processing unit, the brain of the computer? In a way, yes. But not completely.

"The central processing unit's job is to read the programming it is given, interpret it, and carry out its instructions. Without programming, even it would be worthless.

"Give it a program to run, though, and it will bring the rest of the computer online.

"It is the same with your brain, the central processing unit of your body. As Tesla once quipped, 'My brain is only a receiver. In the universe there is a core from which we obtain knowledge, strength, inspiration. I have not penetrated into the secrets of this core, but I know that it exists.'"

6

"You know that your heart beats. Now ask yourself how. What spurred it into existence? What animates it? And how does it know how to beat and at specific rates and rhythms depending on your activities?

"You know that your lungs extract oxygen from the air and expel carbon dioxide. Now ask yourself how. What is It that gives them life and their abilities? How do they know not to absorb carbon dioxide instead and expel oxygen?

"You know that you are conscious. You know that you are aware. Now ask yourself how. How is it that you are conscious? By what means is it that you are aware?

"You may answer that your brain governs consciousness. You may answer that your brain runs your heart and your lungs. But what gives it life and how does it know what to do?

"You may answer that your cells know what to do—that they govern such things. They govern the functions of your brain, your heart, and your lungs. Ask yourself how. What is It that gives them life and instructs them in their activities?

"You may answer that the atoms that create your cells tell them what to do. Ask yourself how. How are these atoms formed and given life? How do they know what to do? How do they know to create cells and which cells to create? How do they know to create brain cells in one area of your body, heart cells in another, and lung cells in another, and then connect them all together?

"The answer is obvious. There *must* be some kind of Intelligence within you that 'codes' for your existence. There must be some sort of energy present that not only creates and animates your 'hardware' but also instructs it. If not, you would not exist or function. Nor would anything else.

"Brahman is the name we have given this Intelligent energy. It is the intelligence of existence in the form of an unfathomable energy that holds within it the 'codes', 'software', or 'programming' of life."

7

"If Brahman is this Intelligence, then what is Atman? And what is the ego?

"Think of Brahman as the base 'operating system' of your 'computer'; That which writes the 'Root Code' or 'DNA' of existence in general.

"Think of Atman as a subroutine—another version of 'software', another 'operating system'— created by Brahman to begin breaking Its general unified 'Code' into individual 'codes', into individual realms, into individual existences, into individual experiences, into individual 'software', into individual DNA.

"Think of the ego as another subroutine, another version of 'software', another 'operating system', one that has been programmed to finalize the separation of the unified code of Brahman into individual experiences, existences, and awarenesses."

8

"The reality you perceive depends on the 'subroutine', the 'software', the 'operating system', the state of mind, through which you perceive it.

"View life through the 'programming' of the ego and you will experience only material existence and individuality, for that is the only 'code' it contains.

"View life through the initial 'programming' of Brahman and you will find no physicality or separation whatsoever.

"View life through the 'programming' of Atman and you will experience a hybrid representation of reality; separation begins to fade and the boundaries of physical existence begin to crumble, but not completely."

9

"What happens to these 'operating systems' at death?

"The superficial 'operating system' of the ego perishes. It is tied to the body and is no longer needed. It only codes for material existence. When you die, it dies, so it is no longer around to interpret reality for you.

"Atman, the intermediate 'system', remains. It either returns you to another body, another ego, or it absorbs your consciousness back into itself.

"If it takes you in, you continue your journey within Its realm. You continue to progress, wading through increasingly ethereal realms, over many more lifetimes, towards your final reunification with Brahman."

10

"How does Atman decide? How does It determine your destination?

"It decides based on your progress within the Game of Life.

"If, at death, you are still using the superficial 'operating system', if you are still attempting to cling to it, then you will be returned to this realm where you will develop another body and another ego.

"If you have 'leveled up', if you have found your way into the intermediate 'software', the intermediate 'operating system', you move on. You become immersed within the 'intermediate code' Itself, the intermediate realms of Atman, where you continue to progress, where you continue to 'level up'.

"There is no judgment, at least in terms of good or bad. The superficial 'operating system' is tied to this realm. If you remain connected to it, you stay here.

"Atman is tied to other realms. Once you 'plug' yourself into Its 'software', you move on.

"Brahman is tied to nothing. Once you 'plug' yourself into It, your journey is complete."

11

"Do you have to wait for death to experience Atman or even Brahman? No, you do not.

"During the deepest states of meditation, prayer, sleep, and suffering, the 'programming' of the ego falters and then fails. Atman, and sometimes Brahman (depending on the depth of your experience), then becomes apparent.

"Near-death experiences allow the same.

"Cease clinging to your ego in your daily life, cease clinging to its 'operating system', and you will have found yet another route.

"One way or another, the 'programming' of the ego must be transcended.

"This is why you are here. This is the 'game' you are here to play. This is the 'puzzle' you are here to unravel."

12

"Because the physical realm, the 'operating system' of the material world, is a duality, separated by the ego's programming into twos—the male and the female, the proton and the electron, the positive and the negative, the yang and the yin—all that exists in the physical world of form is perceived in pairs, from humans down to the smallest of organisms.

"Thus do we experience both hot and cold, left and right, up and down, here and there, hard and soft, day and night, summer and winter, youth and old age, birth and death, male and female, me and you.

"Even our emotions occur in pairs, from happiness to sadness, from courage to fear, and from contentment to frustration.

"We even find duality in many languages, where the words that make up that language are divided into masculine and feminine counterparts.

"For every male there is a female, for every up there is a down, and for every joy there is a corresponding state of despair. But only in this realm. Only while within this 'operating system'."

13

"The overall programming of life has been created in such a way as to project the essence of Brahman, the ethereal DNA of Brahamn, into the physical world of form.

"The material world, and all within It, *is* Its physical form; the culmination of all yang and all yin energies, all positive and all negative charges, all male and all female life forms.

"It is Atman, and ultimately the ego, that breaks the unified 'Code' of existence into the individual parts that we have become so accustomed to."

14

"Observed in parts, the unity of life will easily be missed.

"Only by observing life as a single living Energy, as a single living Entity, as a single living Intelligence, as a single living 'Code', can Brahman be realized."

15

"With the creation of this dual code for physical existence came the desire, inherent within every being, within every force, within every action, and within every emotion, for the two to reunite back into one.

"Each half misses its corresponding partner and is drawn to it. Lost in separation, each half yearns to once again become whole.

"Thus does Brahaman, the root Intelligence, the root 'Coder' of existence, experience and relish a loving, aching exchange between Its two halves.

"This is why we feel alone. This is why we feel troubled. This is why we feel unfulfilled. This is why even happiness does not last—it misses its other half.

"Without our other half, we feel susceptible, fractionated, less than, isolated.

"We yearn for the security of returning to the state of wholeness that is Brahman.

"We do not realize that we are already both sides of the coin, both sides of the 'Code', and thereby suffer.

"Brahman realizes that It is whole and so enjoys the reunion over and over and over again. Knowing separation allows Brahman to more fully experience the joy of reunion.

"This, ultimately, is the purpose of life."

16

"This constant desire, this never-ending yearning, this naturally inherent craving of the positive for its negative counterpart—the yang for its yin, the proton for its electron, testosterone for estrogen, and vice versa—is proof of our need for completion. It is also the impetus for the production of offspring.

"Through this longing are all species and all forces brought together and new life birthed forth.

"Thus is the love of all things for its counterpart the source of both the reproductive urge and the desire for enlightenment."

17

"Most people do not know Atman for they do not know where to look for It. Or how. They are caught up in the duality-based 'code' of material existence. They break down and view all that is in parts.

"They distinguish between a this and a that, between what is up and what is down, between what is left and what is right, between what is before them and what is behind, between what is good and what is bad, between what is me and what is you.

"This is their mistake.

"When viewed in parts, Brahman is incomplete. It cannot be understood in such a manner.

"One must find a way beyond the duality-based 'programming' of the mind to find It. One must come to comprehend the Whole, not seek It within Its isolated parts."

18

"Brahman is both up and down, left and right, before and after, right and wrong, good and bad, male and female, existence and non-existence, me and you.

"Find your way beyond all concepts of duality and there It is—the Soul of the World.

"It created both sides of the coin, both sides of the 'Code'. It *is* both sides."

19

"Think of it this way: a song cannot be absorbed, under-stood, or appreciated from a single note. Nor can a work of art be appreciated from a single brush stroke.

"It is the culmination of all the notes in a song, all the brush strokes in a work of art, that make it a song or a work of art.

"The same goes for Life, the living Intelligence, the ultimate 'Coder', that we refer to as Brahman."

20

"Every aspect of your life, every aspect of all lives ever lived, every aspect of existence as a whole—the good, the bad, and the ugly; the sacred, the holy, and the profane; birth, death, and all that is in between; all that you have seen, heard, and felt, and all that you have not—merge into a single rhythm in the end. A single energy. A single 'Code'. A single vibration. The vibration of Om. The hum of existence. The purr of Brahman. The strum, thrum, and throb of Life. The murmur of the Eternal.

"Heard as individual notes, one can easily discern between the joys of pleasure and the moans of pain.

"Heard as the Song of Creation, in Its totality, as One Voice, one hears only the Om of peace."

21

"Mathematically speaking, put into the vernacular of coding, if all of the pleasures in this realm were to be given a numerical value of 1 and all of the displeasures were to be given a numerical value of -1, the sum total would come to 0.

"If all of the yang aspects of life were to be given a numerical value of 1, and all of the yin aspects of life were to be given a numerical value of -1, the sum total would come, once again, to 0.

"The totality of life exists in a state of balance that is neither pleasure nor pain, yang or yin, up or down, right or left, here or there, before or after, hot or cold, hard or soft, masculine or feminine, aggressive or passive. It is averaged out into a state of imperturbable tranquility.

"It is the 'programming' of the ego, and, to a lesser extent, the 'programming' of Atman, that breaks the singular 'Code of Life' down into parts."

22

"Salt dissolved into water cannot be seen, but it can be tasted—it can be discerned.

"Likewise, the energy that animates the computer cannot be seen, yet its presence is obvious. Without it, you would not be able to turn the computer on.

"The code of the computer program that is being run cannot be seen either, yet its presence is obvious as well. Without it, the application you are attempting to use would not run.

"It is the same with life in general, and with your body specifically. There *must* be an energy source present or else it would not exist. And there *must* be a 'program' present or else it would not run coherently.

"If there is a program, then it stands to reason that there must also be a 'programm*er*'."

23

"Does DNA not hold the 'code' of existence? Is DNA not the 'code' of your being? Is it not the 'software'?

"It is, but what created the DNA? What put the 'code' within it and breathed life into it?"

24

"Cease living life by default! Cease taking the miracle for granted!

"Do not just see objects before you. Ponder the atoms that form and animate those objects. Ponder the source of those atoms. Where do they come from and why do they exist? What gave them their lives? How do they know what to do?

"Ask yourself how it is that life is so unerringly precise. Ask yourself by what adhesive it must be that everything is created, held together, and runs so harmoniously.

"Ponder these questions over and over and over again.

"Ponder these questions until it becomes habitual.

"Ponder these questions until it becomes second nature.

"Ponder these questions until it becomes the default method through which you experience this world.

"Ponder these questions until you burn with desire to uncover the answer.

"Then and only then will the answer become apparent.

"Then and only then will the existence of an Energy, the existence of an Intelligence, the existence of a 'Coder' become obvious, whether you personify It or comprehend It in some other way."

25

"Repeatedly ask yourself how it is that each and every form in this world is created from nothing, held in existence, and then spurred on to perform trillions of interconnected and interrelated functions with every second that goes by.

"If not by some sort of interconnected ever-present Intelligence, then how do you explain it? What other explanation can you come up with?

"Something cannot come from nothing. Existence must come from something. What did it come from? Think! Get to the root of the question!

"Do so and you will begin to realize the miracle of life, the miracle of this Intelligence.

"Realize that this Intelligence *must* exist. Realize that there *must* be some sort of binding Force that holds all there is together and you *will* begin to perceive It."

26

"What is it like to awaken?

"Within the 'operating system' of duality, one sees another, one hears another, one smells another, one speaks to another, one knows another, one thinks of another.

"Within the 'operating system' of Atman, these barriers begin to dissolve.

"Within the 'operating system' of Brahman, they cease to exist altogether. There, you will find nothing outside of your Self to see, hear, smell, speak to, or know of.

"This may seem scary at first, and it is. You are leaving the known and entering the unknown. This transition is known as the 'Dark Night of the Soul'.

"Once you arrive at that far shore though, all fear will leave you. You will know only peace."

27

"When the underlying Intelligence of life first entered into individual form, It seemed to fragment into an almost endless array of atoms, which, as you know, are the building blocks of matter.

"Yet It did not fragment. Not really. This is simply how this Energy, the Light of Consciousness, is projected into this realm.

"Punch as many holes as you can fit into a can, take it into a dark room, and then light a candle within it. The room will be filled with individual streams of light. The walls will be splattered with dots of the same.

"Has the flame, the source of the light itself, fragmented? No. It is still whole. The rips in the fabric through which its emanations travel are what cast the illusion of separation.

"Atman, and to a greater extent the ego, are the rips through which the Light of Consciousness travels into this realm, creating all that you now know."

28

"Put another way, atoms are the sparks of life that are being emitted from the Flame of existence. They carry the heat, the Life Force of the flame, into every aspect of your existence, from the hairs on your head down to the tips of your fingers and toes.

"When the spark loses its heat, your physical vitality diminishes and eventually fades altogether. But know this: nothing can happen to you without Brahman noticing. Not a single hair can go out of place. Not a single emotion can arise.

"It loves you as It loves Itself, for you are Itself. You are Its child. It has created you from Its essence."

29

"As a razor is enclosed within its casing, so too is this Spark encased within every fiber of your being.

"As earthly fire remains hidden until it is brought forth, so too does this Heavenly Flame remain hidden until certain catalysts are able to bring It into awareness.

"I have taught you of these catalysts. The rest is up to you."

30

"This Flame that I speak of, this Energy I speak of, this Intelligence I speak of is nearer than the ego, more dear than a son or a daughter, more precious than a spouse, more valuable than gold.

"Continue to value earthly treasures above all else and your consciousness will remain blind to Its presence. Continue to value earthly treasures above all else and your attention, and therefore your awareness, will remain locked within the 'operational system' of duality.

"Your desire for earthly pleasantries, along with your fear of the unknown, is what binds you to this 'system', this state of mind. Yet earthly possessions are temporary, ephemeral, transient. They can only offer you irritation, frustration, and unfulfillment in the end. Grow tired of them and you will naturally begin to seek 'Something More'. Seek this 'Something More' and you *will* find It. We all do. Each in our own time. Each in our own way.

"We, each and every one of us, eventually grow tired of our current 'mental software'—our current state of mind, our current method of viewing life—and set out to find a 'better way'.

"Find this 'better way' and you will move beyond all concepts of loneliness, all concepts of need, all concepts of death."

31

"Awaken and you will realize that you *are* Atman, and by extension Brahman, the Flame, the Energy, the Intelligence, the 'Coder' of life.

"Awaken, and you will realize that you *are* the sun and the moon, the planets and the stars, the solar system and the Milky Way Galaxy. You carry their ethereal Flame within you.

"Awaken, and you will realize that you *are* each and every human being in existence—every plant and every animal—past, present or future. You will realize that you are an extension of the Flame that codes for their existence as well as your own.

"Awaken and you will feel your Essence within them.

"Awaken and you will feel their Essence within you as well.

"Awaken and you will realize that you are not a single spark, you are the entirety of the Flame of Life Itself."

32

"If you still think of Brahman as something outside of yourself, if you still think, *I am me and you are you*, if you still think, *I have this and you have that*, then you are still observing life from the superficial 'operating system' of the ego.

"Such a mindset is the root of your suffering.

"Experiencing life through the lens of separation creates the illusion of isolation, the illusion of scarcity, the illusion of need, the illusion of want.

"All it takes is a subtle change in your mindset, a subtle change in what you focus your attention upon, to make it all go away.

"As you change the focus of your attention, you change the 'software' through which you view reality."

33

"Is this easy?

    "Yes and no, but it is worth it.

    "Realize your connection; realize that all of life is One; realize that you are not separate; realize that you already have it all; realize that any direction is a good direction and what anguish is there to be had? How could you possibly suffer?"

34

"Remain attached to your individuality, remain attached to your ego, remain attached to its incessant desires and its fate will become your own. Whatever happens to it will happen to you.

"Worldly desires cannot fulfill you. Even if you are able to obtain all the material pleasantries you wish for, you will still not be satisfied—your ego will *always* want more.

"Buy a house and it will want new curtains. Buy new curtains and it will want new carpet. Buy new carpet and it will want a new car. Buy a new car and it will want new tires. Buy new tires and it will want new hubcaps. The ego's thirst is unquenchable.

"Live this way and at death, by the law of Karma, you will be drawn back into this worldly realm by your desires in order to chase them around once again.

"Shed your ego though, shed your worldly desires and replace them with a burning desire for the Infinite, and at death you will step out of your body, your ego, and your Karma, and move on.

"Can you do this? Of course you can. We all do. Each in our own time. Each in our own way. It is but a matter of time."

35

"I have told you quite a bit, yet there is so much more left to tell. Most of it you will have to experience for yourself though, for the reality of existence is beyond the range of thought. It is unthinkable and unspeakable.

"Just how deep can the rabbit hole go? Deeper than you can imagine.

"Even time does not really exist, for example. It is but the measurement of the rate of change in the position of an object compared to itself or another object.

"A day is measured by the time (the rate of change) it takes the earth to spin once on its axis, is it not? A year is measured by the time (the rate of change) it takes for the earth to travel around the sun.

"Move your consciousness beyond the superficial 'operating system' of your ego and the cadence of time will change. It will cease being linear.

"Move your consciousness into the realm of Brahman and time will cease to exist altogether."

36

"How is this possible?

"If time is the measurement of the rate of change in the position of one object in relation to itself or another object, then how *could* time exist within the realm of Brahman?

"First of all, movement does not exist within the realm of Brahman. Brahman is *potential* energy, the *potential* for movement. It is movement that has not yet been made manifest. Without movement, without change, there is nothing to measure. There is no before or after.

"Secondly, there is no position within the realm of Brahman. The All exists within a singularity that is devoid of space. There is no 'here' or 'there' by which one could produce a coordinate. Again, there is nothing to measure.

"Lastly, there are no 'things', no objects within the realm of Brahman. There is only the Infinite unmanifest, the *possibility* of form. Without 'things', there is, once again, nothing to measure.

"Eternity is not an extension of time but a lack of it."

37

"But light moves, and so does fire, do they not? Yet I just compared light and flame to Brahman, which contains no movement.

"Light and flame are also objects, are they not? Yet I just compared light and flame to Brahman, which contains no objects.

"You are correct on both counts. Light and flame do move, and they are both objects, and I did compare Brahman to light and flame.

"Closer to the truth is that the Light of Consciousness, the Flame of Life, comes from Brahman but is not actually Brahman.

"Brahman is the *potential* for the Light of Consciousness to come forth, the *potential* for the Flame of Life to burn.

"When you experience this Light during near-death experiences, or through other means, you are not yet experiencing Brahman, but you are close. It is just on the other side of the Light.

"The Light, you see, is Atman, your Soul."

38

"You are not a slave to reality, your mind determines your reality, and that reality is determined by the 'operating system' you choose to perceive it through.

"You have control. You always have. Just like Dorothy in the *Wizard of Oz*.

"Complete your journey and all that you see will become holy. The Great Scripture of Life will become written up all that you experience. Brahman will lie at your feet.

"Thieves will no longer be thieves, murderers will no longer be murderers, and saints will no longer be saints.

"All life forms will become gods, immortal and impervious, treading along the same journey of self-discovery that you are on. They may all be at different points in their travels, but you will see that they are all on the same path."

"In truth, everything and everyone is a shadow of the Beloved. We search for It here and there, while looking right at It. Sitting by Its side, we ask, 'where, o where, is my Beloved?'"

-Rumi

Chapter Five

1

The master thus summarized his discourse:

2

"This world is ancient, much older than can be fathomed by the human mind.

"As far back as has been recorded, that is but one cycle of many.

"Just as the seasons come and go, so too does physical existence as a whole. It has been created and destroyed over and over and over again.

"This is the rhythm of life. The inbreath and outbreath of Brahman.

"How many times has existence been created and destroyed? As many as the grains of sand upon this earth."

3

"The ultimate truth has been discovered and handed down for eons; lost and regained then lost and regained again.

"The line of teachers that have discovered the truth and then passed it on is vast beyond measure. They have come in every cycle, in every age, in every era, in every culture.

"Some gained their knowledge through near-death experiences, others through periods of great suffering, still others while in the deepest states of meditation and prayer."

4

"Do not make the mistake of thinking that I, or the other teachers you have just heard from, are the only ones to have ever discovered the truth. Do not worship us or build a dogma around our teachings.

"We are not to be revered. The underlying Intelligence of life, and only the underlying Intelligence of life, is to be revered. We are but Its messengers. There is nothing special about us.

"What we have found you too can find and more. You are meant to. It is why you are here."

5

"Focus on us, obsess over us, and you will miss the path that lies before you. You will miss the other teachers, the other lessons that surround you.

"We have given you the outlay of the truth so that you may follow It, not us.

"We have given you the outlay of the truth so that you may recognize it wherever it is found.

"Do not discard the teachings of any who speak this truth, no matter their land of birth, the time period in which they lived, their culture, or the 'religion' of their followers.

"Followers do not always hold true to the ways of their teachers. Do not use them as a gauge.

"All truth, in the end, is the One Truth. It is ever the same no matter where you find It or from whom."

6

"Remember well your impending death so that you may truly live now. Every moment is a blessing. Another day is never guaranteed.

"Act accordingly. Live intentionally. Ponder your existence!"

7

"Fire, earth, water, air, metal, ether; thunder, lightning, clouds; the sky, the earth, the rocks, the sands; thoughts, yearnings, and that which is yearned for, as well as That which thinks and yearns; the solar system, the Milky Way Galaxy; all solar systems, all galaxies, and That which animates them ... it is all the Self. It is all your Soul. It is all Brahman.

"Look around you and within you and perceive the miracle!

"All that you sense, and all that you do not, is holy. All is sacred.

"All is the one Cosmic Body of Brahman, created, animated, destroyed, and recreated by the one Cosmic Soul.

"That which you seek is not 'out there' somewhere. It is the closest, most intimate aspect of your own being.

"This is the essence of the Upanishads."

"There are many paths to the top of the mountain, but the view is always the same."

-Chinese Proverb

Consider Reading Next

- The Chandogya Upanishad 101
  (Book Two of the Hindu Enlightenment Series)
- Or The Bhagavad Gita 101

Author page: amazon.com/author/matthewbarnes

Or consider starting the Egyptian Enlightenment Series, which is similar:
- The Emerald Tablet 101
- The Hermetica 101
- The Kybalion 101

Matthew's "Zennish Series" books can be read in any order, but he meant for them to be read in the following order:
- Tao Te Ching 101
- Albert Einstein, Zen Master
- Tao Te Ching 201
- Jesus Christ, Zen Master
- *Dr. Seuss, Zen Master
- *Willy Wonka, Zen Master
- Mark Twain, Zen Master

You may even enjoy my Investing Series (Zen-vesting).

- Investing 101
- Investing 201
- Again, my investing style is controversial, but I have done *very* well with it. It is based around riding the rhythm of the market.

* *Dr. Seuss, Zen Master* and *Willy Wonka, Zen Master* have been written but may not be able to be published due to copyright issues.

References

If you are interested, check out this article on the universe as a conscious entity:

https://news.yahoo.com/scientists-believe-universe-conscious-215000641.html#:~:text=Some%20scientists%20have%20posited%20that%20the%20thing%20we,fluttering%20inside%20our%20brains%20and%20generating%20conscious%20thoughts.

The following are the sources I used in preparing my rendition. These are my favorite overall translations:

https://hinduwebsite.com/
https://en.wikipedia.org/wiki/Upanishads
https://www.learnreligions.com/the-principal-upanishads-1770572
https://en.wikipedia.org/wiki/Brihadaranyaka_Upanishad#:~:text=Brihadaranyaka%20Upanishad%20literally%20means%20the%20%22Upanishad%20of%20the,refined%20by%20a%20number%20of%20ancient%20Vedic%20scholars.
https://www.swami-krishnananda.org/brhad_00.html
https://www.hindutsav.com/brihadaranyaka-upanishad/

REFERENCES

I used so many references that I ultimately lost track of some. If I left any out, I sincerely apologize.

Letter from the Author

Dear Reader,

Thank you for reading my book! You've made my day!
I would very much like to know what you thought of my book and why. If you have time, please leave me a review on Amazon letting me know your thoughts. It doesn't need to be complex. A word or sentence will do.

Remember that the number of reviews a book gets and the number of stars a book gets can make or break a book on Amazon, so please be kind. It also helps Amazon to know that you think others may benefit from it.

If you have any questions or comments feel free to email me at Dr.MatthewBarnes12@gmail.com.

I promise I will try to respond.

Thank you for spending time with me!

Matthew Barnes

Author Bio

Matthew Barnes is an avid learner who spent his early years in North Carolina. During college, he experienced a stint with depression, which led him to the works of the Eastern philosophers. He started writing simplified versions of the works he was inspired by in response to a friend who was struggling with religion. He hopes his attempts at simplifying the philosophies of ancient spiritual traditions will make them more accessible to Western minds and, in turn, help bring peace to those, like his friend, who have found themselves lost in a world that, at times, seems so devoid of meaning and hope.

PS: Matthew would like the epitaph on his tombstone to read: *Off exploring. Don't wait up.*

To check the progress of his other works, go to: amazon.com/author/matthewbarnes,

or sign up for updates at:

https://forms.aweber.com/form/50/1802384050.htm

Made in United States
Cleveland, OH
12 March 2025

15117410R00135